P. Charney

FLASHMAPS!

THE INSTANT GUIDE TO

Washington

The idea of SINGLE SUBJECT MAPS with related material was conceived by FLASHMAPS Publications in 1967. A single-subject map, color-coded and cross-indexed, has proven to be a useful tool for clearly dispensing information. FLASHMAPS INSTANT GUIDE books are used by both natives and visitors alike to save time, money and energy.

ENJOY WASHINGTON!

RANDOM HOUSE
NEW YORK

W9-CPW-160

EDITOR-IN-CHIEF:
  Toy Lasker
CARTOGRAPHERS:
  Timothy W. Lasker
  Sally Jarman
DIRECTOR of RESEARCH:
  Gladys F. Caterinicchio
WASHINGTON RESEARCH:
  Martha Wells Lewis

© **1975 Random House, Inc.**
Revised 1977, 79, 80, 81, 83, 85, 86, 87

All rights reserved. Except for use in a review, the reproduction or utilization of this work in any form by any electronic, mechanical, or other means, now known or hereinafter invented, including xerography, photocopying, and recording, and in any information storage and retrieval system, is forbidden without the written permission of Random House, Inc., 201 E. 50th St., New York, N.Y. 10022.

Every effort has been made to assure the accuracy and objectivity of all information in this book, but neither the authors nor the publishers make any warranty, nor assume any responsibility with respect thereto.

"FLASHMAPS", "INSTANT GUIDE", the Grid Design on the front cover of this book, Address Finder, National Treasure, Strollers Map are trademarks of Random House.

Library of Congress Card No. 75-6206
ISBN 0-942226-02-X
Manufactured in The United States of America

CONTENTS

IMPORTANT TELEPHONE NUMBERS
(DC Area Code 202)

Police	911	U.S. Secret Service	535-5100
Fire & Rescue	911	U.S. Park Police	426-6600
Ambulance	911	Alcohol/Drug Hotline	727-0474
Police Dept Info	727-1000	Animal Bites	576-6665
Fire Dept Headquarters	462-1762	Deaf Emergency	727-9334
Poison Control Center	625-3333	Utilities Complaints	727-3065
Suicide Prevention	727-3622	VD Hotline	832-7000
Children's Protection	727-0995	Water & Sewer	673-6600
Civil Defense	727-6161	D C General Hospital	675-5000
Coast Guard	426-2158	Tipster's Confidential	393-2222
FBI	324-3000	Rape & Assault	333-7273

RECORDED INFORMATION

Daily Tourist Info	789-7000	National Archives	523-3000
Dial-A-Museum	357-2020	Passport Office Info	783-8200
Dial-A-Park	426-6975	Ticketron	659-2601
Dial-A-Phenomenon	737-8855	Time of Day	844-2525
Dial-A-Prayer	347-4341	Weather	936-1212
D C Recreation Dept	673-7660	U.S. Weather	655-4000

SERVICES

Abandoned Auto Disposal	673-6993	Marriage License	727-1870
Aging	724-5626	Medicaid	724-5173
Air Pollution	426-2675	Metro Information	637-7000
Business Information	637-7000	Metrobus Lost Property	637-1195
Consumer Complaints	727-7065	Motor Vehicles	727-6680
D C Government	727-1000	National Parks	655-4000
Federal Info	647-4000	Planned Parenthood	347-8500
Food Stamps	727-0858	Telegrams	737-4260
Garbage & Trash	727-4825	Travelers' Aid	661-8638
Human Services	724-5466	U S Capitol	224-3121
Income Tax—D C	727-6103	U S Postal Service	245-4000
Federal	488-3100	White House Tour Info	456-7041
IVIS Translation Service	783-6540	Zoo Info	673-4800

AIRLINES INTO NATIONAL & DULLES AIRPORTS

Air France	*237-2747	Northwest	737-7333
American	393-2345	Ozark	347-4744
American Eagle	393-2345	Pan American	845-8000
Braniff	272-6433	Peoples Express	683-0960
British Airways	393-5300	Piedmont	620-0400
Colgan Airways	631-9060	Republic	347-0448
Continental	628-6666	TWA	887-1870
Delta	468-2282	United	893-3400
Eastern	393-4000	USAir	783-4500
Midway	621-5700	Western	*843-9378
New York Air	588-2300	Wheeler	*334-5890

TERMINALS

Andrews AFB	981-9111	Dulles Airport	471-4242
Balt-Wash Arprt	261-1000	Washington Arprt	557-1155
AMTRAK	Union Station		484-7540
Gray Line Tours	4th & E St SW		479-5975
Greyhound Terminal	1110 New York Ave NW		565-2662
Trailways Bus Terminal	12th & New York Ave NW		737-5800
Tourmobile	1000 Ohio Dr SW		554-7950

*(800) Toll Free

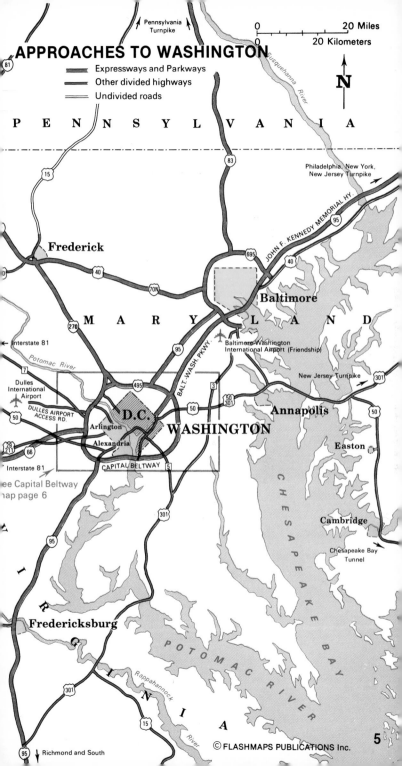

APPROACHES TO WASHINGTON

Expressways and Parkways
Other divided highways
Undivided roads

20 Miles
20 Kilometers

N

P E N N S Y L V A N I A

Susquehanna River

Pennsylvania Turnpike

Philadelphia, New York, New Jersey Turnpike

JOHN F. KENNEDY MEMORIAL HY.

Frederick

Baltimore

M A R Y L A N D

Baltimore-Washington
International Airport (Friendship)

← Interstate 81

Potomac River

New Jersey Turnpike →

Dulles International Airport

DULLES AIRPORT ACCESS RD.

D.C.

Arlington

WASHINGTON

Annapolis

Alexandria

Easton

← Interstate 81

CAPITAL BELTWAY

ee Capital Beltway
ap page 6

C H E S A P E A K E   B A Y

Cambridge

Chesapeake Bay Tunnel →

Fredericksburg

V   I   R   G   I   N   I   A

P O T O M A C   R I V E R

Rappahannock River

↓ Richmond and South

© FLASHMAPS PUBLICATIONS Inc.

5

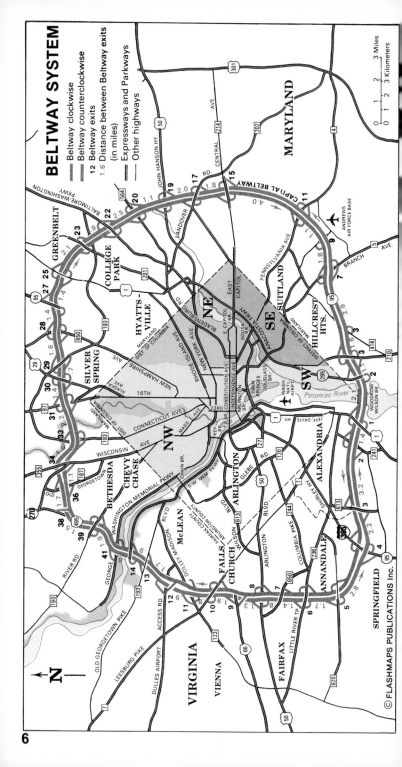

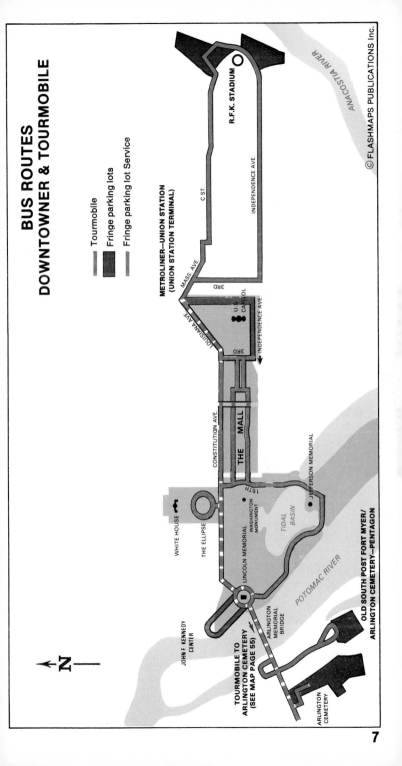

BUS ROUTES
DOWNTOWNER & TOURMOBILE

Tourmobile
Fringe parking lots
Fringe parking lot Service

© FLASHMAPS PUBLICATIONS Inc.

7

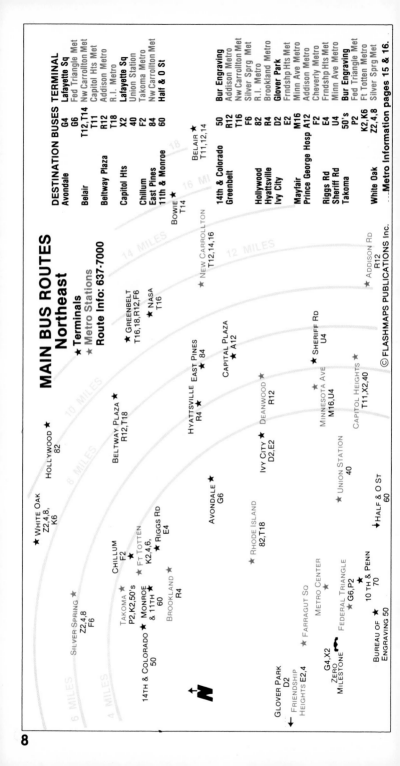

MAIN BUS ROUTES
Southeast

★ Terminals
★ Metro Stations
Route Info: 637-7000

DESTINATION	BUSES	TERMINAL
Andrews AFB	J12	Addison Metro
	K12	Potomac Metro
Bellevue	A4	Archives
Congress Heights	A2	Archives
District Heights	V12	Potomac Metro
	J12	Addison Metro
DC General	96	McLean Gardens
	B2	Anacostia
	B4	Fort Stanton
Fairfax Village	K12, W6	Potomac Metro
	V12	Addison Metro
Garfield	92	Duke Ellington Brdg
Hillcrest	36	Friendship Hts Metro
Livingston	A6, A8	Archives
Marlow Hgts	D12	Federal Ctr Metro
	C12, C14	Potomac Metro
Minnesota Ave	V6	Bur Engraving
	X2	Lafayette Square
Naylor Garden	34	Friendship Hts Metro
Oxon Hill	W12	Federal Ctr Metro
Ridge Rd	V4	Bur Engraving
RFK Stadium	42	Mt. Pleasant
	40	Union Station
Shipley Terrace	32	Friendship Hts Metro
Stanton Rd	94	Duke Ellington Bridge
Temple Hill	H12	Potomac Metro

Metro Information pages 15 & 16.

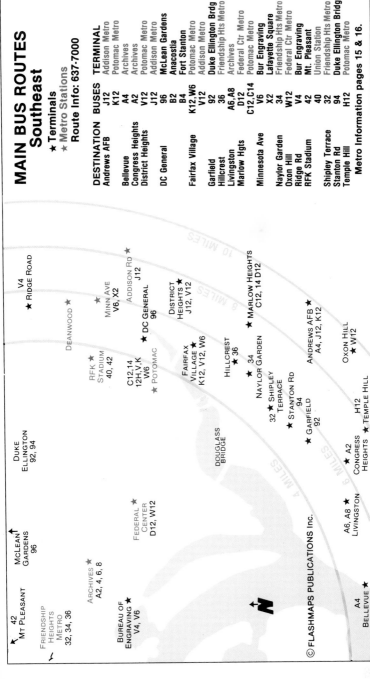

★ MT PLEASANT
42

FRIENDSHIP
HEIGHTS
METRO
32, 34, 36

McLEAN
GARDENS
96

DUKE
ELLINGTON
92, 94

DEANWOOD ★

V4
★ RIDGE ROAD

MINN AVE
V6, X2

ADDISON RD
J12

DISTRICT
HEIGHTS ★
J12, V12

★ DC GENERAL
96

ARCHIVES ★
A2, 4, 6, 8

BUREAU OF
ENGRAVING ★
V4, V6

FEDERAL
CENTER ★
D12, W12

RFK ★
STADIUM
40, 42

C12,14
12H,Y,K
W6
★ POTOMAC

FAIRFAX
VILLAGE ★
K12, V12, W6

HILLCREST
★ 36

★ MARLOW HEIGHTS
C12, 14 D12

★ 34
NAYLOR GARDEN

DOUGLASS
BRIDGE

32 ★ SHIPLEY
TERRACE
STANTON RD
94

★ GARFIELD
92

H12
★ TEMPLE HILL

ANDREWS AFB ★
A4, J12, K12

OXON HILL
★ W12

★ A2
CONGRESS
HEIGHTS

A6, A8 ★
LIVINGSTON

A4
★ BELLEVUE

© FLASHMAPS PUBLICATIONS INC.

10 MILES
8 MILES
4 MILES

N

9

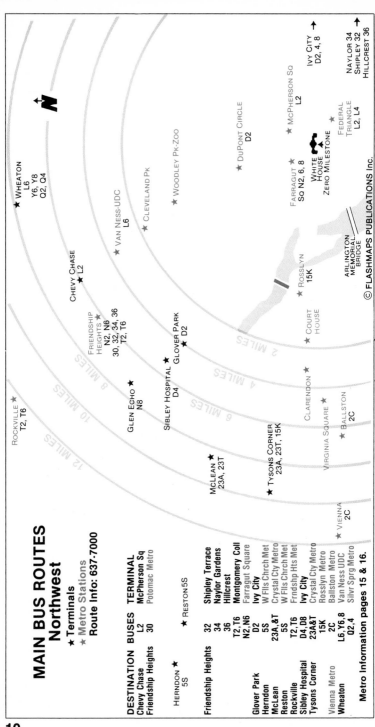

MAIN BUS ROUTES
Northwest

★ Terminals
★ Metro Stations
Route Info: 637-7000

DESTINATION	BUSES	TERMINAL
Chevy Chase	L2	McPherson Sq
Friendship Heights	30	Potomac Metro

★ HERNDON 5S

★ RESTON 5S

Friendship Heights	32	Shipley Terrace
	34	Naylor Gardens
	36	Hillcrest
	T2,T6	Montgomery Coll
	N2,N6	Farragut Square
Glover Park	D2	Ivy City
Herndon	5S	W Flls Chrch Met
McLean	23A,&T	Crystal Cty Metro
Reston	5S	W Flls Chrch Met
	T2,T6	Frndshp Hts Met
Rockville	D4,D8	Ivy City
Sibley Hospital	23A&T	Crystal Cty Metro
Tysons Corner	15K	Rosslyn Metro
		Ballston Metro
Vienna Metro	2C	
Wheaton	L6,Y6,8	Van Ness UDC
	Q2,4	Silvr Sprg Metro

Metro Information pages 15 & 16.

Map labels:
ROCKVILLE ★ T2, T6
WHEATON L6 Y6, Y8 Q2, Q4
FRIENDSHIP HEIGHTS ★ N2, N6 30, 32, 34, 36 T2, T6
CHEVY CHASE ★ L2
VAN NESS-UDC L6
CLEVELAND PK
WOODLEY PK-ZOO
DUPONT CIRCLE D2
McPHERSON SQ L2
FARRAGUT SQ N2, 6, 8
WHITE HOUSE ZERO MILESTONE
FEDERAL TRIANGLE L2, L4
IVY CITY D2, 4, 8
NAYLOR 34 SHIPLEY 32 HILLCREST 36
GLEN ECHO ★ N8
SIBLEY HOSPITAL ★ D4
GLOVER PARK ★ D2
McLEAN ★ 23A, 23T
TYSONS CORNER ★ 23A, 23T, 15K
ROSSLYN 15K
COURT HOUSE
CLARENDON
VIRGINIA SQUARE
BALLSTON ★ 2C
VIENNA ★ 2C
ARLINGTON MEMORIAL BRIDGE

2 MILES
4 MILES
6 MILES
8 MILES
10 MILES
12 MILES

N

© FLASHMAPS PUBLICATIONS Inc.

10

MAIN BUS ROUTES
Southwest

★ Terminals
★ Metro Stations
Route Info: 637-7000

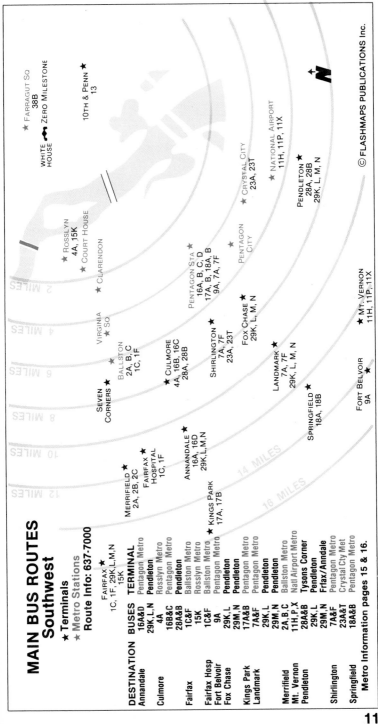

★ FARRAGUT SQ
38B

WHITE HOUSE 〰 ZERO MILESTONE

★ 10TH & PENN
13

★ ROSSLYN
4A, 15K

CRYSTAL CITY ★
23A, 23T

COURT HOUSE

CLARENDON

VIRGINIA SQ

PENTAGON STA ★
16A, B, C, D
17A, B, 18A, B
9A, 7A, 7F

PENTAGON CITY

NATIONAL AIRPORT ★
11H, 11P, 11X

PENDLETON ★
28A, 28B
29K, L, M, N

BALLSTON ★
2A, B, C
1C, 1F

CULMORE ★
4A, 16B, 16C
28A, 28B

SHIRLINGTON ★
7A, 7F
23A, 23T

FOX CHASE ★
29K, L, M, N

LANDMARK ★
7A, 7F
29K, L, M, N

MT. VERNON ★
11H, 11P, 11X

SEVEN CORNERS ★

MERRIFIELD ★
2A, 2B, 2C

FAIRFAX ★
1C, 1F

FAIRFAX HOSPITAL ★
1C, 1F

ANNANDALE ★
16A, 16D
29K, L, M, N

KINGS PARK ★
17A, 17B

SPRINGFIELD ★
18A, 18B

FORT BELVOIR ★
9A

★ FAIRFAX
1C, 1F, 29K, L, M, N
15K

© FLASHMAPS PUBLICATIONS Inc.

DESTINATION	BUSES	TERMINAL
Annandale	16A&D	Pentagon Metro
	29K, L, N	Pendleton
Culmore	4A	Rosslyn Metro
	16B&C	Pentagon Metro
	28A&B	Pendleton
Fairfax	1C&F	Ballston Metro
	15K	Rosslyn Metro
Fairfax Hosp	1C&F	Ballston Metro
Fort Belvoir	9A	Pentagon Metro
Fox Chase	29K, L	Pendleton
	29M, N	Pendleton
Kings Park	17A&B	Pentagon Metro
Landmark	7A&F	Pentagon Metro
	29K, L	Pendleton
	29M,N	Pendleton
Merrifield	2A, B, C	Ballston Metro
Mt. Vernon	11H,P,X	Natl Airport Metro
Pendleton	28A&B	Tysons Corner
	29K, L	Pendleton
	29M,N	Frfax/Anndale
Shirlington	7A&F	Pentagon Metro
	23A&T	Crystal Cty Met
Springfield	18A&B	Pentagon Metro

Metro Information pages 15 & 16.

11

METRO BUS & RAIL TO IMPORTANT CENTERS

Center	Bus Route	Map Pg	Metro	Metro Stop
Carter Barron Amph	5's	10	Red	Silver Spring
Catholic Univ	80, 81, H2, H4	8	Red	Brookland
Chevy Chase Mazza	T6,30's, N2, N6	10	Red	Friendship Hgts
Convention Center	60, 70, K4	8	Blue/Red/Orn	Metro Center
Crystal City	none	11	Blue	Crystal City
DC Armory	42, 96	9	Blue/Orange	Stadium/Armory
Gallaudet College	92,94,D2,D4,D8	8		
Greyhound	60,K4,D2,D4,D8	9	Blue/Org/Red	Metro Center
Hospitals:				
Capitol Hill	92,94	8	Blue/Orange	Capitol South
Childrens	H2, H4	10	Red	Brookland
Columbia	30's	10	Blue/Orange	Foggy Bottom
DC General	96,98,B2,B4,B5	9	Red/Orange	Stdium/Armory
Fairfax	1C,1F,26T	11	Orange	Ballston
Georgetown Univ	D4	10	Red	DuPont Circle
Geo Washington U	30's	10	Blue/Orange	Foggy Bottom
Hadley	A4	11	Blue/Orange	Federal Center
Howard Univ	70's,G2	8	Red	Gallery/DuPont Circle
Prince George	A12,F2	8	Orange	Landover/Cheverly
Providence	80, 81	8	Red	Brookland
Psychiatric Instit	D4	10	Red	Dupont Circle
St. Elizabeth's	A's	9	Blue/Orange	Federal Center
Southeast Comm	A2	9	Blue/Orange	Federal Center
Sibley	D4	10	Red	DuPont Circle
Walter Reed	S2, S4, 70's	8	Red	Silver Spring
Washington Center	H2, H4	8	Red	Brookland
V.A.	H2, H4	8	Red	Brookland
Howard University	70's, G2	8	Red	Gallery/DuPont
Ivy City	D2, D4, E2	8	Red	Union Sta/Ft Totten
Kennedy Center	46,81	10	Red	DuPont Circ/Metro Ctr
Landmark	29K, L, M, N	11	Yellow	King Street
Landover Mall	A12	8	Orange	Landover
Marine Barracks	52,54,92,94	9	Blue/Orange	East Market
Montgomery Mall	J2, J3	10	Red	Medical Center
NASA Greenbelt	T16	11	Orange	New Carrollton
National Airport	11H, 11P, 11X	11	Blue/Yellow	National Airport
National Shrine	80,81,H2/4G4/6	8	Red	Brookland
Naval Observatory	N2, N4, N6	10	Red	DuPont Circle
Naval Ordinance Lab	K6	8	Red	Brookland
Naval Research Lab	A4, A5	9	Blue/Orange	Federal Center
Navy Annex	16's	11	Blue/Yellow	Pentagon
Navy Yard	52,54,92,94,	9	Blue/Orange	East Market
Pentagon	16's, 17's,8's	11	Blue/Yellow	Pentagon
Prince George Plaza	F4, F6, R2	8	Red	Silver Spr/Brklnd
RFK Stadium	42, 96	9	Blue/Orange	Stadium/Armory
Reston, VA	5's	10	Orange	West Falls Church
Seven Corners	1's	10	Orange	Ballston
Springfield	18's, 26T	11	Blue/Orge	Pentagon/Dunn Loring
Trailways Bus	96	9	Red	Union Station
Tysons Corner	5S, 28A & B	10	Orange	West Falls Church
Union Station	40, 42, D's, 96	8	Red	Union Station
Univ of DC	L2, L4, L6	8	Red	Van Ness
Univ Maryland	82,83,R2	8	Red	Brookland/R.I.
Washington Cathedral	30's, N2, N6	10	Red	Friendship Heights
White Flint	70's, G2	10	Red	White Flint
Zoo	L's	10	Red	Woodley Pk Zoo

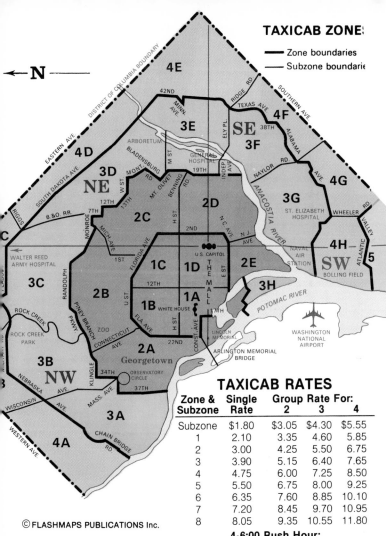

TAXICAB ZONES

← **N** ─

━ Zone boundaries
─ Subzone boundaries

© FLASHMAPS PUBLICATIONS Inc.

TAXICAB RATES

Zone & Subzone	Single Rate	Group Rate For: 2	3	4
Subzone	$1.80	$3.05	$4.30	$5.55
1	2.10	3.35	4.60	5.85
2	3.00	4.25	5.50	6.75
3	3.90	5.15	6.40	7.65
4	4.75	6.00	7.25	8.50
5	5.50	6.75	8.00	9.25
6	6.35	7.60	8.85	10.10
7	7.20	8.45	9.70	10.95
8	8.05	9.35	10.55	11.80

**4-6:00 Rush Hour:
$1.00 surcharge.**

Rates change between zones and subzones.
Two or more passengers:
  Same destination—group rate
  Different destination—single rate
  Children five and under: no charge
Airport Fare: Dulles—$27.00 to $32.00   National—$6.00 to $9.00
  Luggage: One piece free per person. 15¢ each additional.
Telephone called taxi: $.65 extra.
Messenger service: Same rate as single passenger.
Trunks: in excess of 34'' x 18'' x 9'' or three cubic feet—$1.25 each.
Waiting rate: 75¢ for each 5 minutes up to 45 minutes.
Hourly rate: First hour or fraction thereof: $12.00
  Additional 15 minutes—$3.00
Handicapped passengers: No extra charge for aids or Seeing Eye dogs.

13

METRO STATIONS—ALPHABETICAL

Metro Stop	Approximate Location	Metro Line	Fringe Parking
Addison Road	Central Ave Addison Rd, MD	Blue	551
Archives	Penn Ave & 7th NW, DC	Yellow	
Arlington Cemetery*	Memorial Dr & Jeff Davis, VA	Blue	
Ballston*	Fairfax Blvd & N Stuart St, VA	Orange	
Benning Rd	E Capitol & Benning Rd NE, DC	Blue	
Bethesda	Wisconsin at Montgomery Ln, MD	Red	
Braddock Rd	Braddock Rd & West St, VA	Yellow	
Brookland-CUA	Michigan Av & Bunker Hill Rd N-E, DC	Red	
Capitol Heights	E Capitol & Southern Ave, MD	Blue	336
Capitol South	1st St betw C / D Sts SE, DC	Blue/Orange	
Cheverly	Columbia Pk Rd & Cheverly, MD	Orange	496 & Midday
Clarendon*	Wilson Blvd & N Highland St, VA	Orange	
Cleveland Park*	Porter/Ordway & Conn, DC	Red	
Court House*	Wilson Blvd / Uhle St, VA	Orange	
Crystal City*	18th St betw Clark & Jeff Davis, VA	Blue/Yellow	
Deanwood	Minn Ave betw Nash & 48th St, MD	Orange	191 & Midday
Dunn Loring*	Gallows Rd & I-66, VA	Orange	1050
Dupont Circle*	Conn & Q / 19th St, DC	Red	
Eastern Market*	Penn Ave & 7th St SE, DC	Blue/Orange	
Eisenhower Ave	Eisenhower Ave & RR Sta, VA	Yellow	
Falls Church, East*	I-66 N Sycamore St, VA	Orange	365
Falls Church, West*	I-66 at Leesburg Pke VA	Orange	1000
Farragut North*	Conn & L/Conn & K Sts NW, DC	Red	
Farragut West*	Eye & 17th /Eye & 18th Sts, DC	Blue/Orange	
Federal Center*	D St & 3rd, DC	Blue/Orange	
Federal Triangle*	12th & Penn / Constitution, DC	Blue/Orange	
Foggy Bottom (GWU)*	Eye St & 23rd NW, DC	Blue/Orange	
Fort Totten	Galloway St at RR, DC	Red	330 & Midday
Friendship Heights	Western Ave & Wisconsin, DC	Red	
Gallery Place*	7th & G/7th & H/ 9th & G NW	Red/Yellow	
Grosvenor	Rockville Pke & Grosvenor, MD	Red	614
Huntington	Huntington Ave & Kings Hwy, VA	Yellow	2282
Judiciary Square*	F & 4th - 5th/D-E & 4th, NW	Red	
King Street	King St & Commonwealth, VA	Yellow	
Landover	Penn Dr & N of Landover, MD	Orange	1131 & Midday
L'Enfant Plaza*	D & 9th/D & 6-7th/Md & 7th, SW	Blu/Or/Yell	
McPherson Square*	Eye & 14th/Vermont & Eye, DC	Blue/Orange	
Medical Center	Rockville Pike & South Dr, MD	Red	
Metro Center*	G & 11th, 12th, 13th, F & 12th	Red/Blu/Orng	
Minnesota Ave	Minn & Grant St NE, DC	Orange	263 & Midday
National Airport	North Term & Smith Blvd, VA	Blue/Yellow	
New Carrollton	79th Ave & RR Sta, MD	Orange	1552 & Midday
Pentagon*	Pentagon concourse/Metrobus Is, VA	Blue/Yellow	
Pentagon City*	Hayes Rd betw Army/Navy & 15th, VA	Blue/Yellow	800 (private)
Potomac Ave*	14th St & Potomac Ave SE	Blue/Orange	
Rhode Island Ave	RI Ave & 8th St NE (RR Sta), DC	Red	322 & Midday
Rockville	Hungerford Dr (355) & Park Rd, MD	Red	518
Rosslyn*	N Moore St & 19th / Wilson, VA	Blue/Orange	
Shady Grove	Rt 355 & Redland Rd, MD	Red	3149
Silver Spring	Colesville betw E/W hwy & Wayne, Md	Red	537
Smithsonian*	12th & Indep/12th & Jefferson, SW	Blue/Orange	
Stadium Armory*	19th St & C/19th & Indep, SE	Blue/Orange	2000 (stadium)
Takoma	Carroll Ave & Cedar St NW, DC	Red	100 & Midday
Tenleytown	Wisconsin & Albermarle Av NW, DC	Red	
Twinbrook	Halpine Rd & RR Sta, MD	Red	
UDC-Van Ness	Van Ness & Conn NW, DC	Red	
Union Station*	Union Station (1st & Mass), NE	Red	
Vienna*	Nutley St & I-66, VA	Orange	2135
Virginia Square*	Fairfax & N Monroe, VA	Orange	
White Flint	Marinelli Rd & Rockville Pke, MD	Red	933
Zoological Park	Conn & 24th/Woodley NW, DC	Red	

*Underground station with elevator   Midday parking: 10 AM to 3 PM

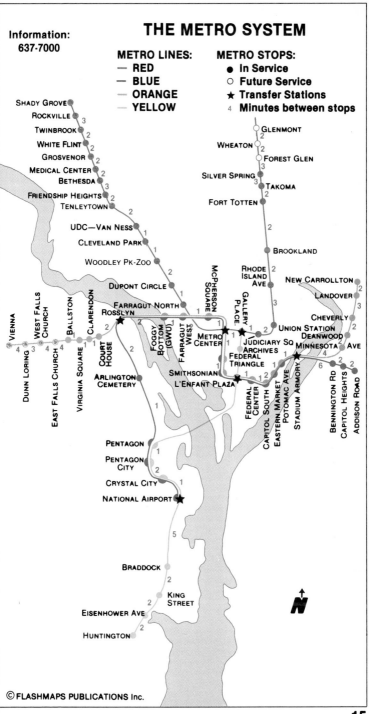

THE METRO SYSTEM

© FLASHMAPS PUBLICATIONS Inc.

15

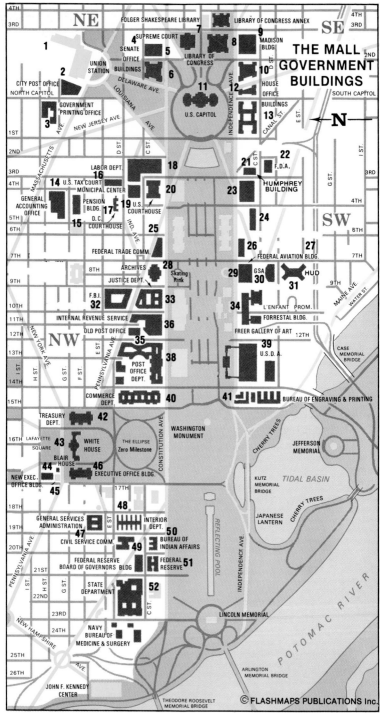

THE MALL
GOVERNMENT
BUILDINGS

NE

SE

SW

NW

N

1. Union Station
2. City Post Office
3. Government Printing Office
4. Supreme Court
5. Senate Office Buildings
6.
7. Folger Shakespeare Library
8.
9. Madison Bldg.
10. House Office Buildings
11. U.S. Capitol
12.
13.
14. U.S. Tax Court
15. D.C. Courthouse
16. Labor Dept.
17.
18.
19. U.S. Courthouse
20.
21.
22. F.D.A.
23. Humphrey Building
24.
25.
26.
27.
28. Archives
29.
30. GSA
31. HUD
32. F.B.I.
33.
34.
35.
36.
37.
38.
39. U.S.D.A.
40. Commerce Dept.
41. Bureau of Engraving & Printing
42. Treasury Dept.
43. White House
44. Blair House
45. New Exec. Office Bldg.
46. Executive Office Bldg.
47. General Services Administration
48.
49. Civil Service Comm.
50. Interior Dept.
51. Federal Reserve
52. State Department

Folger Shakespeare Library
Library of Congress Annex
Supreme Court
Senate Office Buildings
Library of Congress
Madison Bldg.
House Office Buildings
U.S. Capitol
Labor Dept.
U.S. Tax Court
Municipal Center
General Accounting Office
Pension Bldg.
D.C. Courthouse
U.S. Courthouse
F.D.A.
Humphrey Building
Archives
Justice Dept.
Skating Rink
Federal Trade Comm.
Federal Aviation Bldg.
GSA
HUD
L'Enfant Prom.
Forrestal Bldg.
Freer Gallery of Art
U.S.D.A.
Internal Revenue Service
Old Post Office
Post Office Dept.
Commerce Dept.
Bureau of Engraving & Printing
Treasury Dept.
Lafayette Square
White House
The Ellipse
Zero Milestone
Blair House
Executive Office Bldg.
New Exec. Office Bldg.
Washington Monument
General Services Administration
Interior Dept.
Civil Service Comm.
Bureau of Indian Affairs
Federal Reserve Board of Governors Bldg
Federal Reserve
State Department
Navy Bureau of Medicine & Surgery
Reflecting Pool
Lincoln Memorial
Jefferson Memorial
Tidal Basin
Kutz Memorial Bridge
Japanese Lantern
Cherry Trees
Case Memorial Bridge
Potomac River
Arlington Memorial Bridge
Theodore Roosevelt Memorial Bridge
John F. Kennedy Center

© FLASHMAPS PUBLICATIONS Inc.

16

MALL GOVERNMENT BUILDINGS—BY MAP NUMBER

MALL GOVERNMENT BUILDINGS—ALPHABETICAL

ARCHITECTURAL LANDMARKS

Building	Architect	Date	Map Page
Arts & Industries	Cluss & Schultze	1880	18
Blair—Lee House	Unknown	1824	16
Botanical Gardens	Bennett, Parson, Frost	1902	18
Bureau of Engraving	James G. Hill	1880	16
Capitol	Wm. Thornton & Latrobe	1829	16
Constitution Hall	John Russell Pope	1930	18
Corcoran Gallery of Art	Ernest Flagg	1897	18
Decatur House	Benjamin Latrobe	1818	18
DC Courthouse	George Hadfield	1850	16
DC Government Building	Cope & Stewardson	1908	16
Dulles Internat'l Airport	Eero Saarinen	1962	5
Executive Office	A. B. Mullett	1888	16
Hirshhorn Museum	Gordon Bundshaft	1974	18
John F Kennedy Center	Edward Durell Stone	1969	18

(Continued) **17**

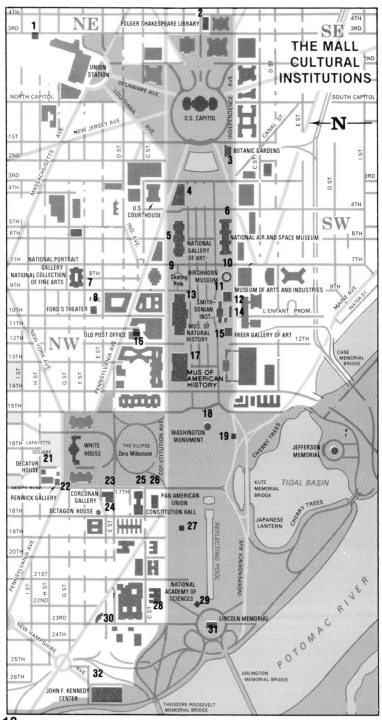

THE MALL
CULTURAL
INSTITUTIONS

NE
SE
SW
NW
N

4TH
3RD
2ND

FOLGER SHAKESPEARE LIBRARY

1

2

UNION STATION

DELAWARE AVE.
NORTH CAPITOL
NEW JERSEY AVE.
LOUISIANA AVE.
MASSACHUSETTS AVE.

U.S. CAPITOL

INDEPENDENCE AVE.
CANAL ST
SOUTH CAPITOL
E ST

1ST
2ND
3RD
4TH
5TH
6TH

D ST
C ST
IND. AVE.

BOTANIC GARDENS

3

C ST
G ST

4

U.S. COURTHOUSE

5

6

NATIONAL GALLERY OF ART

NATIONAL AIR AND SPACE MUSEUM

7TH

NATIONAL PORTRAIT GALLERY
NATIONAL COLLECTION OF FINE ARTS

9

Skating Rink

HIRSHHORN MUSEUM

10

11

MUSEUM OF ARTS AND INDUSTRIES

7

8TH
9TH
10TH
11TH
12TH
13TH

FORD'S THEATER

8

F.T.

OLD POST OFFICE

16

13

SMITH-SONIAN INST.

MUS. OF NATURAL HISTORY

12

14

15

FREER GALLERY OF ART

L'ENFANT PROM.

MAINE AVE.
WATER ST

CASE MEMORIAL BRIDGE

17

MUS OF AMERICAN HISTORY

14TH
15TH
16TH

LAFAYETTE SQUARE

WHITE HOUSE

21

DECATUR HOUSE

18

19

WASHINGTON MONUMENT

THE ELLIPSE
Zero Milestone

CONSTITUTION AVE.

CHERRY TREES

JEFFERSON MEMORIAL

TIDAL BASIN

KUTZ MEMORIAL BRIDGE

RENWICK GALLERY

22

CORCORAN GALLERY

OCTAGON HOUSE

23

24

25 26

17TH

PAN AMERICAN UNION
CONSTITUTION HALL

JAPANESE LANTERN

CHERRY TREES

18TH
19TH
20TH
21ST
22ND
23RD
24TH

PENNSYLVANIA AVE.
NEW YORK AVE.
I ST
H ST
G ST
F ST
E ST

27

REFLECTING POOL

INDEPENDENCE AVE.

POTOMAC RIVER

28

NATIONAL ACADEMY OF SCIENCES

29

30

31

LINCOLN MEMORIAL

25TH
26TH

NEW HAMPSHIRE AVE.

32

JOHN F. KENNEDY CENTER

ARLINGTON MEMORIAL BRIDGE

THEODORE ROOSEVELT MEMORIAL BRIDGE

18

MALL CULTURAL INSTITUTIONS—BY MAP NUMBER

MALL CULTURAL INSTITUTIONS—ALPHABETICAL

ARCHITECTURAL LANDMARKS (Continued)

Building	Architect	Date	Map Page
Jefferson Memorial	John Russell Pope	1943	18
Library of Congress	Smithmeyer & Pelz	1897	16
Lincoln Memorial	Henry Bacon	1922	18
Martin Luther King Library	Mies Van der Rohe	1972	68
National Air & Space Mus.	Gyo Obata	1976	18
Nat'l Gallery Art-East Wing	I. M. Pei	1978	18
Nat'l Gallery Art-West Wing	John Russell Pope	1941	18
National Geographic Society	Edward Durrell Stone	1964	76
Octagon House	Dr. William Thornton	1800	18
Old Pension Building	Gen. Montgomery Meigs	1883	16
Old Post Office	W. Edbrooke	1899	16
Pan American Health	Roman Fresnedo-Siri	1964	16
Pan American Union	Al Kelsey, Paul Cret	1910	16
Phillips Gallery	Hornblower, Marshall	1897	18
Portrait Gallery	Wm. Elliott R. Mills	1867	18
Pre-Columbian Museum	Philip Johnson	1963	76
Renwick Gallery	James Renwick	1859	18
Smithsonian	James Renwick	1849	18
Supreme Court	Cass Gilbert	1935	16
Treasury	R.Mills, T.V. Walter	1869	16
Washington Monument	Robert Mills	1885	18
White House	J.Hoban,Benjamin Latrobe	1792	16
Union Station	Daniel H. Burnham	1908	16
Vietnam Vets' Wall/Statue	Maya Ying Lin/Frank Hart	1984	18

Church	Date	Architect	Church	Date	Architect
All Souls Unitarn	1924	Coolidge/Shattuck	Metropolitan AME	1885	Samuel Morsell
Christ Church	1805	Benj H Latrobe	St John's	1816	Benjamin Latrobe
Friends Meetng House	1930	Walter Price	St Mary's Episc	1887	Renwick, Aspinwall
Holy Trinity Parish	1851	Francis Stanton	St Matthew's Cath.	1899	Heines/LaFarge
Luther Memorial	1870	Judson York	Washington Cath.	1907	Philip H Frohman

FOR CHURCH LOCATIONS PAGE 52

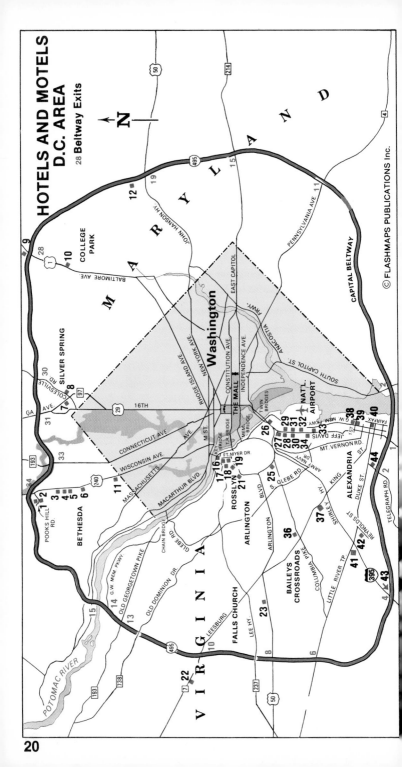

HOTELS AND MOTELS
D.C. AREA
28 Beltway Exits

N

© FLASHMAPS PUBLICATIONS Inc.

20

HOTELS & MOTELS D.C. AREA—BY MAP NUMBERS

1 Marriott	11 Holiday Chevy	26 Marriott Tw Br	36 Spring Hill
2 Linden Hill	12 Sheraton N. C.	27 Quality Pntgn	37 Radisson
3 Ramada Bthsd	16 Marriott Ky Br	28 Marriott Gate	38 Ramada Old
4 American Inn	17 BW Westpark	29 Holiday Arprt	39 BW Old Colny
5 Holiday Bthsd	18 Hyatt Key Brd	30 Days Inn	40 Holiday Inn
6 Bethesdan	19 Holiday Rslyn	30 Embassy Suites	40 Morrison Hse
7 Holiday Slv Sp	21 Quality Inn	31 Marriott Crys	41 Days Inn
8 Sheraton Silvr	22 Marriott-Tysons	32 Stouffers	42 Guest Qrters
9 Holiday Bltwy	23 Quality Gov	33 Hyatt Crystal	43 Hilton Inn
10 Days Inn U Md	25 Sheraton Natl	34 Howard Johnsn	44 Holiday Tel

HOTELS & MOTELS D.C. AREA—ALPHABETICAL

Hotel/Motel (Room Rate) ★	Address	Map No	Telephone	Rooms
American Inn (c)	8130 Wisconsin Ave, Bthesda	4	(301) 656-9300	72
BW Old Colony Inn (b)	N Washington & 1st	39	(703) 548-6300	223
BW Westpark (b)	1900 N Ft Meyer Dr, Rosslyn	17	(703) 527-4814	307
Bethesdan (c)	7740 Wisconsin Ave, Bethsda	6	(301) 656-2100	73
Days Inn (c)	I-395 & Rt 236, W Alexandria	41	(703) 354-4950	200
Days Inn Arlington (c)	2000 Jeff Davis Hwy, Arl	30	(703) 920-8600	250
Days Inn-U of Md (c)	9137 Baltimore Blvd	10	(301) 345-5000	68
Embassy Suites (a+)	1300 Jeff Davis Hwy, Arl	30	(703) 979-9799	267
Guest Quarters (a)	100 S Reynolds, Alexandria	42	(703) 370-9600	215
Hilton Inn Sprngfld (b+)	6550 Loisdale Court	43	(703) 971-8900	246
Holiday Inn-Airport (b+)	1489 Jeff Davis Hwy, Arlngtn	29	(703) 521-1600	308
Holiday Inn-Beltway (b)	10,000 Baltimore, College Pk	9	(301) 345-6700	123
Holiday Inn-Bethesda (b)	8120 Wisconsin Ave, Bethsda	5	(301) 652-2000	267
Holiday Inn-Chvy Chs (b)	5520 Wisconsin Ave	11	(301) 656-1500	223
Holiday Inn-Old Town (a)	480 King St, Alex	40	(703) 549-6080	228
Holiday Inn-Telegraph (b)	2460 Eisenhower Ave, Alex	44	(703) 960-3400	260
Holiday Inn-Rosslyn (b)	1850 N Ft Meyer Dr	19	(703) 522-0400	178
Holiday Inn-Silver Spr (c)	8777 Georgia Ave	7	(301) 589-0800	231
Howard Johnson's (b+)	2650 Jeff Davis Hwy, Arl	34	(703) 684-7200	275
Hyatt Key Bridge (a+)	1325 Wilson Blvd	18	(703) 841-9595	303
Hyatt Reg Cryst Cty (a+)	2799 Jeff Davis Hwy, Arl	33	(703)486-1234	693
Linden Hill Hotel (c)	Pooks Hill Rd, Bethesda	2	(301) 530-0300	300
Marriott-Cryst Cty (a+)	1999 Jefferson Davis Hwy	31	(703) 521-5500	301
Marriott Gateway (a+)	1700 Jeff Davis Hwy, Arlngtn	28	(703) 920-3230	454
Marriott Bethesda (a+)	5151 Pooks Hill Rd, Bethesda	1	(301) 897-9400	410
Marriott-Key Bridge (a+)	1401 Lee Hwy, Rosslyn	16	(703) 524-6400	558
Marriott-Twin Bridges (a)	US 1 & I-95, Arlington	26	(703) 628-4200	447
Marriott-Tys Crnr (a+)	8028 Leesburg Pike	22	(703) 734-3200	393
Morrison House (a+)	116 S Alfred, Alex (Old Town)	40	(703) 838-8000	47
Quality Inn-Arlingt (b)	Arlington Blvd & Courthse, Arl	21	(703) 524-4000	363
Quality Inn-Governor (c)	6650 Arlington Blvd, Falls Ch	23	(703) 532-8900	123
Quality Inn-Pentagon (a)	300 Army Navy Dr, Arlington	27	(703) 892-4100	635
Radisson Mark Plz (a+)	5000 Seminary Rd, Alex	37	(703) 845-1010	428
Ramada Inn-Old Town (a)	901 N Fairfax, Alexandria	38	(703) 683-6000	255
Ramada Inn-Bethesda (a)	8400 Wisconsin Ave	3	(301) 654-1000	144
Sheraton Hotel (b)	8500 Annapolis Rd, New Carrll	12	(301) 459-6700	250
Sheraton-Wash NW (b)	8727 Colesville Rd, Slv Spg	8	(301) 589-5200	283
Sheraton National (a)	Columbia Pk & Wash Blvd, Arl	25	(703) 521-1900	431
Spring Hill Lodge (c)	5666 Columbia Pk, Bailys Crs	36	(703) 820-5600	60
Stouffers Cncourse (a+)	2399 Jeff Davis Hwy, Arl	32	(703) 979-6800	400

*ROOM RATES (DOUBLE): (a) $90-115   (b) $70-90   (c) $40-70   **21**

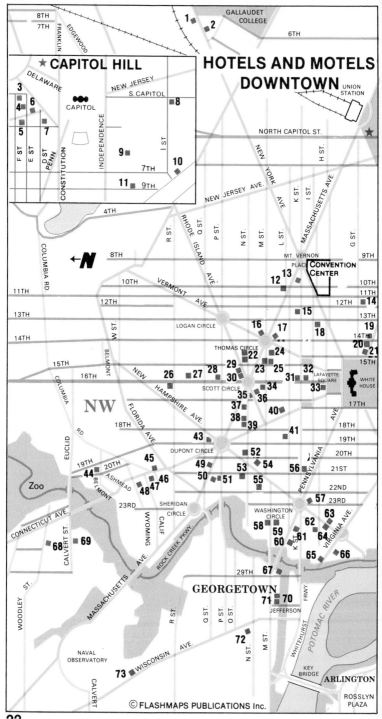

HOTELS AND MOTELS
DOWNTOWN

★ CAPITOL HILL

GALLAUDET COLLEGE

UNION STATION

CAPITOL

CONVENTION CENTER

LAFAYETTE SQUARE

WHITE HOUSE

Zoo

NW

Washington CIRCLE

DUPONT CIRCLE

LOGAN CIRCLE

THOMAS CIRCLE

SCOTT CIRCLE

SHERIDAN CIRCLE

GEORGETOWN

NAVAL OBSERVATORY

POTOMAC RIVER

KEY BRIDGE

ARLINGTON

ROSSLYN PLAZA

© FLASHMAPS PUBLICATIONS Inc.

22

DOWNTOWN HOTELS & MOTELS—BY MAP NUMBER

1 BW Regency	25 Madison Hotel	51 Georgetown Omni
2 BW Envoy	26 Windsor Inn	52 Ramada Renaissnce
3 Phoenix Park	27 Embassy Inn	53 Hampshire Hotel
4 Bellevue Hotel	28 Quality Inn D'twn	54 Embassy Square
5 Sheraton Grand	29 Holiday Inn Central	55 Marriott Washington
6 Quality Inn Capitol	30 Park Terrace	56 Lombardy Hotel
7 Hyatt Regency	31 Capital Hilton	57 One Washington Cir
8 BW Skyline	32 Sheraton Carlton	58 Park Hyatt
9 Holiday Capital	33 Hay Adams Hotel	59 Grand Hotel
10 Channel Inn	34 Jefferson Hotel	59 Westin International
11 Loew's L'Enfant Plz	35 Holiday Inn D'twn	60 Guest Quarters
12 Morrison-Clark	36 Gramery Inn	61 Bristol Hotel
13 Henley Park	37 Canterbury Hotel	62 River Inn
14 Harrington Hotel	38 Tabard Inn	63 Guest Quarters
15 BW Convention	39 Gralyn, The	64 Inn Foggy Bottom
16 Washington Plaza	40 Mayflower Hotel	65 Ho Jo Kennedy
17 Holiday Inn Thos Cir	41 Anthony	66 Watergate
18 Youth Hostel	43 DuPont Plaza	67 Four Seasons
19 Marriott, J. W.	44 Rock Creek	68 Sheraton Washington
20 Willard Hotel	45 Washington Hilton	69 Shoreham Omni
21 Hotel Washington	46 Highland Hotel	70 Georgetown Marbury
22 General Scott	47 Holiday Inn Conn	71 Georgetown Dutch
22 Ramada Inn Central	48 Normandy Inn	72 Georgetown Inn
23 Dolley Madison	49 Embassy Row	73 Holiday-Georgetown
24 Vista International	50 Ritz Carlton	

DOWNTOWN HOTELS & MOTELS—ALPHABETICAL

Hotel/Motel (Room Rate) ★	Address	Map No.	Telephone	Rooms
Anthony Hotel (b)	1823 L Street NW	41	223-4320	100
Bellevue Hotel (b)	15 E Street NW	4	638-0900	280
Best Western Envoy (c)	501 New York Ave NE	2	543-7400	73
BW Convention Ctr (c)	12th & K Street, NW	15	842-1020	218
BW Regency Congress (c)	600 New York Ave NE	1	546-9200	50
BW Skyline Inn (c)	10 Eye Street SW	8	488-7500	203
Bristol Hotel (a)	2430 Penn Ave NW	61	955-6400	240
Canterbury Hotel (a)	1733 N Street NW	37	393-3000	99
Capital Hilton (a)	16th & K Street NW	31	393-1000	534
Channel Inn (b)	650 Water Street SW	10	554-2400	100
Dolley Madison, The (a)	1507 M Street NW	23	862-1876	42
DuPont Plaza (b)	DuPont Circle	43	483-6000	312
Embassy Inn (c)	1627 16th Street NW	27	234-7800	41
Embassy Row (a)	2015 Mass Ave NW	49	265-1600	194
Embassy Square (b)	2000 N Street, NW	54	659-9000	213
Four Seasons (a+)	2800 Penn Ave NW	67	342-0444	198
General Scott Inn (c)	1464 Rhode Island Ave	22	333-6700	65
Georgetown Dutch Inn (b)	1075 Thos Jefferson NW	71	337-0900	54
Georgetown Inn (a)	1310 Wisconsin NW	72	333-8900	95
Georgetown Marbury (b)	3000 M Street, NW	70	726-5000	164
Georgetown Omni (a)	2121 P Street NW	51	293-3100	300
Gralyn, The (c)	1745 N Street NW	39	785-1515	34
Gramercy Inn (b)	1616 Rhode Island NW	36	347-9550	320
Grand Hotel, The (a)	2350 M Street NW	59	429-0100	263
Guest-Quarters (b)	801 New Hampshire NW	63	785-2000	101
Guest Quarters (b)	2500 Penn Ave NW	60	333-8060	123
Hampshire Hotel (b)	1310 New Hampshire	53	296-7600	82
Harrington Hotel (c)	11th & E Street NW	14	628-8140	300
Hay-Adams (a+)	800 16th Street NW	33	638-6600	165
Henley Park Radisson (a)	926 Mass Ave NW	13	638-5200	98

★ROOM RATES (DOUBLE): (a) $160-190   (b) $90-160   (c) $60-85   **23**

DOWNTOWN HOTELS & MOTELS Continued

Hotel/Motel (Room Rate) ★	Address	Map No.	Telephone	Rooms
Highland Hotel (b)	1914 Conn Ave NW	46	797-2000	140
Holiday-Capitol (b)	550 C Street SW	9	479-4000	529
Holiday Inn-Central (c)	1501 Rhode Island NW	29	483-2000	214
Holiday Inn-Conn Ave (c)	1900 Conn Ave NW	47	332-9300	145
Holiday Inn-Downtown (b)	1615 Rhode Island NW	35	296-2100	161
Holiday Inn-Georgetown (c)	2101 Wisconsin NW	73	338-4600	147
Holiday Inn-Thomas Cir (c)	Mass & Thomas Circle	17	737-1200	207
Hotel Washington (b)	15th St & Penn Ave NW	21	638-5900	350
Ho Jo Kennedy Center (b)	2601 Virginia NW	65	965-2700	190
Hyatt Regency (a)	400 New Jersey NW	7	737-1234	842
Inn at Foggy Bottom (b)	824 New Hampshire	64	337-6620	96
Jefferson Hotel (a)	16th Street & M NW	34	347-2200	104
Loew's L'Enfant Plaza (a)	480 l'Enfant Plaza	11	484-1000	373
Lombardy Hotel (b)	2019 Eye Street NW	56	828-2600	122
Madison Hotel (a)	15th Street & M NW	25	862-1600	362
Marriott Washington (a)	1221 22nd Street NW	55	872-1500	350
Marriott, J. W. (a)	1331 Penn Ave NW	19	393-2000	774
Mayflower Hotel (a +)	1127 Conn Ave NW	40	347-3000	720
Morrison-Clark Inn (a)	Massachusetts & L St	12	462-9107	54
Normandy Inn (c)	2118 Wyoming NW	48	483-1350	77
One Washington Circle (a)	1 Washington Circle NW	57	872-1680	150
Park Hyatt (a)	1201 24th Street NW	58	789-1234	233
Park Terrace Hotel (b)	1515 Rhode Island NW	30	232-7000	189
Phoenix Park (a)	520 N Capitol NW	3	638-6900	87
Quality Inn-Capitol (b)	415 New Jersey NW	6	638-1616	350
Quality Inn Downtown (b)	1315 16th Street NW	28	232-8000	135
Ramada Inn Central (b)	1430 Rhode Island	22	462-7777	186
Ramada Renaissance (b)	1143 New Hampshire	52	775-0800	360
Ritz Carlton (a +)	2100 Mass Ave NW	50	835-2100	260
River Inn Hotel (b)	924 25th Street NW	62	337-7600	128
Rock Creek (c)	1925 Belmont NW	44	462-6007	52
Sheraton-Carlton (a)	16th Street & K NW	32	638-2626	218
Sheraton Grand (a)	New Jersey Ave & F St	5	628-2100	265
Sheraton-Washington (b)	2660 Woodley NW	68	328-2000	1505
Shoreham Hotel Omni (a)	2500 Calvert NW	69	234-0700	800
Tabard Inn (b)	1739 N Street NW	38	785-1277	40
Vista International (a)	1400 M Street NW	24	429-1700	413
Washington Hilton (b)	1919 Conn Ave NW	45	483-3000	1150
Washington Plaza (b)	Mass & Thomas Circle	16	842-1300	343
Watergate Hotel (a +)	2650 Virginia Ave NW	66	965-2300	238
Westin Washington DC (a)	M Street & 24th NW	59	429-2400	400
Willard Intercontinental (a +)	1401 Penn Ave	20	628-9100	390
Windsor Inn (c)	1842 16th Street NW	26	667-0300	89
Youth Hostel (c)	1332 Eye Street NW	18	347-3125	175

*ROOM RATES (DOUBLE): (a) $160-190   (b) $90-160   (c) $60-85

CAPITOL HILL & WATER FRONT RESTAURANTS
BY MAP NUMBERS — Map page 25

1 Hawk & Dove
2 Toscanni
3 Taverna Greek
4 Jenkin's
4 Stevan's
5 209½
6 Cafe Capri
7 La Brasserie

8 Monocle
9 Hunan's
10 Anton's
11 Bullfeathers
12 Powerscourt
13 La Colline
14 Kelly's Irish Times
15 Hugo's

15 Jonah's
16 Market Inn
17 Apple of Eve
18 Phillip's Flgshp
19 Hogate's
20 700 Water St
21 Pier 7
22 Gangplank

24

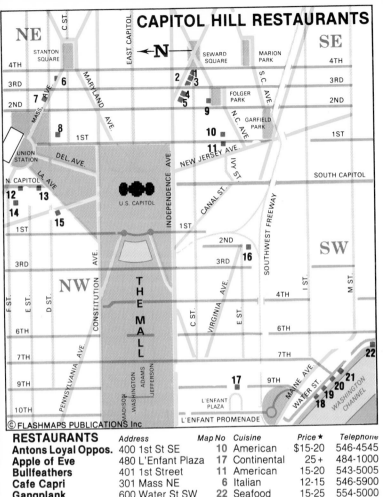

CAPITOL HILL RESTAURANTS

RESTAURANTS	Address	Map No	Cuisine	Price ★	Telephone
Antons Loyal Oppos.	400 1st St SE	10	American	$15-20	546-4545
Apple of Eve	480 L'Enfant Plaza	17	Continental	25+	484-1000
Bullfeathers	401 1st Street	11	American	15-20	543-5005
Cafe Capri	301 Mass NE	6	Italian	12-15	546-5900
Gangplank	600 Water St SW	22	Seafood	15-25	554-5000
Hawk & Dove	329 Penn SE	1	American	10-15	543-3300
Hogate's	9th St & Maine SW	19	Seafood	15-25	484-6300
Hugo's	400 New Jersey NW	15	Continental	25-30	737-1234
Hunan Capitol Hill	201 D St NE	9	Hunan/Szech	11-15	544-0102
Jenkin's Hill	223 Penn SE	4	American	10-14	544-6600
Jonah's Seafood	400 New Jersey NW	15	Seafood	40-50	737-1234
Kelly's Irish Times	14 F St NW	14	American	10-15	543-5433
La Brasserie	239 Mass NE	7	French	18-25	546-9154
La Colline	400 N Capitol NW	13	French	15-20	737-0400
Market Inn	200 E St SW	16	Seafood	12-20	554-2100
Monocle	107 D St NE	8	American	15-25	546-4488
Phillip's Flagship	900 Water St SW	18	Seafood	12-18	488-8515
Pier 7	650 Water St SW	21	Seafood/Stk	15-25	554-2500
Powerscourt, The	520 N Capitol NW	12	Irish Contl	20-35	737-3776
700 Water Street	700 Water St SW	20	American	12-20	554-7320
Stevan's on Hill	231 Penn SE	4	American	11-15	543-8337
Taverna Greek Isles	307 Penn SE	3	Greek	8-15	547-8360
Toscanini's	313 Penn Ave SE	2	Italian	10-18	544-2338
209½	209½ Penn SE	5	American	20-30	544-6352

★ Prices do not include drinks or gratuities

25

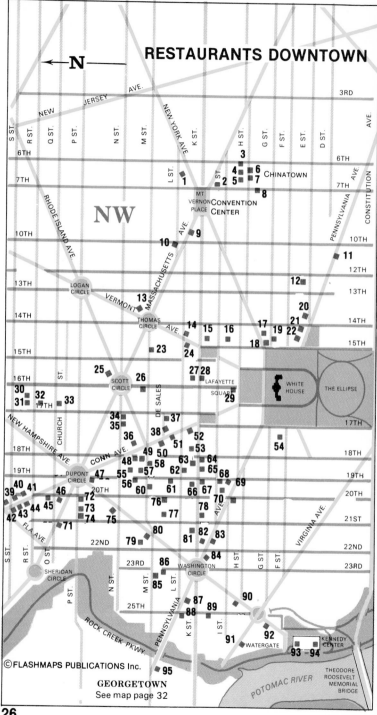

RESTAURANTS DOWNTOWN

← N →

3RD

NEW JERSEY AVE.

S ST. R ST. Q ST. P ST. N ST. M ST. NEW YORK AVE. K ST. H ST. G ST. F ST. E ST. D ST.

6TH 6TH
7TH 7TH

RHODE ISLAND AVE.

NW

3
1 **4** **6** CHINATOWN
2 **5** **7**
8

MT VERNON Convention
PLACE Center

PENNSYLVANIA AVE.

CONSTITUTION

10TH **9** 10TH
10 **11**

MASSACHUSETTS AVE.

12TH **12** 12TH
LOGAN CIRCLE
VERMONT **13** 13TH
13TH **20**
14TH **14 15 16** **17 19** **21** 14TH
THOMAS CIRCLE **18** **22**
AVE. **23 24**
15TH **23** 15TH

16TH **25** **27 28** 16TH
SCOTT CIRCLE **26** LAFAYETTE
30 **32** SQUARE **29**
31 **33**
17TH

WHITE HOUSE THE ELLIPSE

DE SALES

CHURCH

NEW HAMPSHIRE AVE.

CONN. AVE.

34 **37**
35
36 **38** 17TH
18TH **51 52** 18TH
48 49 50 53 **54**
19TH **47 55 57 58 63 64** 19TH
DUPONT **56 60 62 65 68**
CIRCLE **61 66 67 69**
20TH **39 40 41** 20TH
46 72 **76 78 70**
42 43 44 45 **73 77**
74 75
21ST **71** **80** 21ST
FLA AVE. **79** **81 82 83**

VIRGINIA AVE.

22ND **22ND**
84
23RD **86** 23RD
WASHINGTON CIRCLE
SHERIDAN CIRCLE **85**
87 90
88 89
91 92
WATERGATE
93 94 KENNEDY CENTER

ROCK CREEK PKWY.

©FLASHMAPS PUBLICATIONS Inc.
95
GEORGETOWN
See map page 32

POTOMAC RIVER

THEODORE ROOSEVELT MEMORIAL BRIDGE

26

DOWNTOWN RESTAURANTS—BY MAP NUMBERS

1 A. V. Ristorante	32 Paramount	63 Bombay Palace
2 Szechuan	33 Boss Shepherds	64 Cafe Sorbet
3 Ruby	34 Chaucer's	65 Shezan
4 China Inn	35 Iron Gate Inn	66 Tiberio
5 China Doll	36 Joe & Mo's	67 House of Hunan
6 Big Wong	37 Nicholas	68 Charlie Chiang's
7 Hunan's Chinatown	38 Charlie's Crab	69 Dominique's
8 Golden Palace	39 Ruth Chris	70 Devon Bar & Grill
9 Coeur de Lion	40 Anna Maria's	70 La Maree
10 Morrison-Clark	41 Fourways	71 Jockey Club
11 Blossoms	42 Katmandu	72 Nanking
11 Cafe Maxine	43 Cafe Petitto	73 Galileo
11 Fitch Fox	43 Food for Thought	74 Bootsie, Winky
11 Hunan Pavilion	43 Tokyo Sukiyaki	75 Lafitte
12 Dankers	44 Odeon	76 Marrocco's
13 American Harvest	45 Childe Harold	77 Il Giardino
14 Lenny's	45 Vincenzo's	78 Prime Rib
15 Jacques	46 La Reserve	79 Blackie's House
16 Peking	47 DuPont Garden	80 Giorgio's Tartufo
17 Old Ebbitt Grill	48 Cantina d'Italia	81 Mr. K's
18 Prime Plus	49 Astor	82 Le Gaulois
19 Skyroom	50 Le Lion d'Or	83 Trieste
20 Celadon	51 Mel Krupin's	84 West End Cafe
21 Willard Room	52 Duke Ziebert's	85 Le Jardin
22 Occidental	52 Le Pavilion	86 Mayfair, The
23 Montpelier Room	53 Harvey's	87 Bristol Grill
24 Empress Trudie	54 Maison Blanche	88 Cantina Mexicano's
25 Chardonnay	55 Palm, The	89 Foggy Bottom
26 Hunt Club	56 Bread Oven	90 Intrigue, The
27 Trader Vic	56 Sichuan Garden	91 Jean-Louis
27 Twig's	57 Gusti's	91 Wintergarden
28 Carlton Room	58 Gary's	92 Les Champs
29 John Hay Room	60 Jacqueline's	93 Roof Terrace
30 El Bodegon	61 Luigi's	94 Curtain Call
31 La Fonda	62 Jean Pierre	95 Aux Beaux Champs

DOWNTOWN RESTAURANTS—ALPHABETICAL

Restaurant	Address	Map No.	Cuisine	Avg Dinner Price ★	Telephone
American Harvest	Vista Internatl Hotel	13	American	$25-35	429-1700
Anna Maria's	1737 Conn NW	40	Italian	10-15	667-1444
Astor	1813 M St NW	49	Greek	8-14	331-7994
Aux Beaux Champs	2800 Penn Ave NW	95	French	30 +	342-0810
A.V. Ristorante	607 New York NW	1	Italian	10-20	737-0550
Big Wong	610 H St NW	6	Chinese	10-12	638-0116
Blackie's Hse of Beef	22nd St & M NW	79	American	15-20	333-1100
Blossoms	Old PO Pavilion	11	American	10-20	371-1838
Bombay Palace	1835 K St NW	63	No. Indian	12-15	331-0111
Bootsie Winky Maud	2026 P St NW	74	American	10-20	887-0900
Boss Shepherds	1527 17th St NW	33	No. Italian	10-15	328-8193
Bread Oven	1220 19th St NW	56	French	10-20	466-4264
Bristol Grill	Bristol Hotel	87	American	35 +	955-6400
Cafe Maxine	Old PO Pavilion	11	French	20-25	289-8464
Cafe Petitto	1724 Conn Ave NW	43	Italian	10-15	462-8771
Cafe Sorbet	1810 K St NW	64	French	5-10	293-3000

★ Prices do not include drinks or gratuities

Restaurant	Address	Map No.	Cuisine	Avg Dinner Price ★	Telephone
Cantina d'Italia	1214A 18th St NW	48	Italian	$50+	659-1830
Cantina Mexicano's	2512 L St NW	88	Mexican	10-18	342-5644
Carlton Room	Sheraton Carlton Htl	28	Continental	35+	638-2626
Celadon	J W Marriott Hotel	20	Fr/Oriental	20-25	393-2000
Chardonnay	Park Terrace Hotel	25	New Amer	25-30	232-7000
Charlie Chiang's	1912 Eye St NW	68	Chinese	10-20	293-6000
Charlie's Crab	1101 Conn NW	38	Seafood	10-20	785-4505
Chaucer's	Canterbury Hotel	34	Continental	20-30	296-0665
Childe Harold	1610 20th St NW	45	American	15-20	483-6702
China Doll	627 H St NW	5	Szechuan	7-10	842-0660
China Inn	631 H St NW	4	Chinese	7-10	842-0909
Coeur de Lion	Henley Pk Hotel	9	French	35+	638-5200
Curtain Call Cafe	2700 F St NW	94	American	16-20	833-8870
Dankers	1209 E St NW	12	American	10-15	628-2330
Devon Bar & Grill	2000 Penn Ave NW	70	Seafood	13-20	833-5660
Dominique's	1900 Penn Ave	69	French	20-30	452-1126
Duke Ziebert's	1050 Conn Ave NW	52	Steak/Seafd	20-30	466-3730
Dupont Garden	1333 N Hampshire	47	Cant/Szech	15-18	296-6500
El Bodegon	1637 R St NW	30	Spanish	10-18	667-1710
Empress, Trudie	1018 Vermont NW	24	Chinese	25-35	737-2324
Fitch, Fox, & Brown	Old PO Pavilion	11	Cont Amer	10-20	289-1100
Foggy Bottom Cafe	River Inn Hotel	89	American	10-18	338-8707
Food For Thought	1738 Conn Ave NW	43	Vegetarian	8-12	797-1095
Fourways Restaurant	1701 20th St NW	41	French	55+	483-3200
Galileo	2014 P St NW	73	Italian	25-30	293-7191
Gary's	1800 M St NW	58	American	35+	463-6470
Giorgio's Tartufo	1200 N Hampshire	80	No. Italian	18-40	887-5489
Golden Palace	720 7th St NW	8	Cantonese	10-18	783-1225
Gusti's	1837 M St NW	57	Italian	10-15	331-9444
Harvey's	1001 18th St NW	53	Seafood	20-25	833-1858
House of Hunan	1900 K St NW	67	Chinese	12-20	293-9111
Hunans Chinatown	624 H St NW	7	Hunan/Szch	20-25	783-5858
Hunan at Pavilion	Old PO Pavilion	11	Chinese	8-10	371-2828
Hunt Club	Jefferson Hotel	26	European	30-35	467-4849
Il Giardino	1110 21st St NW	77	Italian	35+	223-4555
Intrigue, The	824 New Hampshire	90	No. Italian	10-15	333-2266
Iron Gate Inn	1734 N St NW	35	Mid East	10-15	737-1370
Jacqueline's	1990 M St NW	60	French	25-30	785-8877
Jacques	915 15th St NW	15	French	20-25	737-4445
Jean-Louis	Watergate Hotel	91	French	50+	298-4488
Jean-Pierre	1835 K St NW	62	French	40+	466-2022
Jockey Club	Ritz Carlton Htl	71	Continental	45+	659-8000
Joe & Mo's	1211 Conn Ave	36	Steak	35+	659-1211
John Hay Room	Hay Adams Hotel	29	French	30-35	638-6600
Katmandu	1800B Conn Ave	42	Nepali	15-20	483-6470
Lafitte	1310 N Hampshire	75	Creole	10-20	296-7600
La Fonda	1639 R St NW	31	Mexican	8-12	232-6965
La Maree	1919 Eye St	70	French	40+	659-4447
La Reserve	2015 Mass NW	46	Continental	25-30	265-1600
Le Gaulois	2133 Penn NW	82	French	20-30	466-3232
Le Jardin	1113 23rd St NW	85	French	10-15	457-0057
Le Lion d'Or	1150 Conn NW	50	French	50+	296-7972
Le Pavillon	1050 Conn NW	52	Fr Nouvlle	35+	833-3846

★ *Prices do not include drinks or gratuities*

DOWNTOWN RESTAURANTS Continued

Restaurant	Address	Map No.	Cuisine	Avg Dinner Price ★	Telephone
Lenny's	1025 Vermont NW	14	Continental	$10-15	638-1313
Les Champs	600 New Hampshire	92	Continental	15-20	298-4477
Luigi's	1132 19th St NW	61	Italian	8-12	331-7574
Maison Blanche	1725 F St NW	54	French	35+	842-0070
Marrocco's	1120 20th St NW	76	Italian	12-20	331-9664
Mayfair, The	Grand Hotel	86	Continental	50+	955-4488
Mel Krupin's	1120 Conn NW	51	American	35+	331-7000
Montpelier Room	Madison Hotel	23	Amer/Contl	35+	862-1712
Morrison-Clark Inn	Mass Ave & L St	10	American	20-25	462-9107
Mr. K's	2121 K St NW	81	Chinese	40-50	331-8868
Nanking	2002 P St NW	72	Chinese	7-10	785-2208
Nicholas	Mayflower Hotel	37	American	25-35	347-8900
Occidental	1475 Penn Ave NW	22	Reg Amer	10-15	639-8718
Odeon	1714 Conn Ave NW	44	Italian	10-15	328-6228
Old Ebbitt Grille	675 15th St NW	17	American	20-25	347-4800
Palm, The	1225 19th St NW	55	American	35+	293-9091
Paramount Steakhse	1609 17th St NW	32	Steak	10-14	232-0395
Peking	823 15th St NW	16	Chinese	8-12	737-4540
Prime Rib	2020 K St NW	78	American	35+	466-8811
Prime Plus	727 15th St NW	18	Nouvlle Amer	35+	783-0166
Roof Terrace	Kennedy Center	93	Continental	15-25	833-8870
Ruby	609 H St NW	3	Chinese	8-10	842-0060
Ruth's Chris Stkhse	1801 Conn Ave NW	39	Steak	18-30	797-0033
Shezan	913 19th St NW	65	Indian	20-25	659-5555
Szechuan	615 Eye St NW	2	Chinese	10-15	393-0130
Sichuan Garden	1220 19th St NW	56	Sichuan	17-25	296-4550
Skyroom	Hotel Washington	19	Fr Contl	25-35	347-4499
Tiberio	1915 K St NW	66	Italian	35+	452-1915
Tokyo Sukiyaki	1736 Conn NW	43	Japanese	10-15	462-7891
Trader Vic's	Capital Hilton Hotel	27	Seafood	25-30	347-7100
Trieste	2138½ Penn Ave	83	Italian	10-12	338-8444
Twigs	Capital Hilton Hotel	27	American	15-20	393-1000
Vincenzo's	1606 20th St NW	45	Seafood	30+	667-0047
West End Cafe	1 Wash Circle Hotel	84	Continental	20-25	293-5390
Willard Room	Willard Hotel	21	American	35+	628-9100
Wintergarden	Watergate Hotel	91	International	25+	298-4455

★ Prices do not include drinks or gratuities

OTHER DINING IN D.C. AND AREA

DINNER THEATERS

	Address	Telephone
Burn Brae	Rte 29 Black Burn Rd, Burtonsville, Md	(301) 384-5800
Colony 7	Rte 32 & Baltimore/Washington Pkwy	(301) 953-2370
dc space	7th Street & E, Washington DC	(202) 347-4960
Harlequin	1330 Gude Dr, Rockville, Md	(301) 340-8515
Hayloft	10501 Balls Ford Rd, Manassas, Va	(703) 631-0230
Lazy Susan Inn	Woodbridge, Virginia	(703) 550-7384
Little Theater	600 Wolfe Street, Alexandria, VA	(703) 683-0496
Petrucci's Main St	312 Main St, Laurel, Md	(301) 725-5226
Round House Thea	12210 Bushey Dr, Silver Spring, MD	(301) 468-4234
Toby's Dinner Thea	Route 29, Columbia, Md	(301) 730-8311
West End Dinner	4615 Duke St, Alex, Va	(703) 370-2500

POTOMAC CRUISE DINING

Potomac River Cruise	Zero Prince St, Alexandria, Va	(703) 683-6076
Washington Boat Line	Pier 4, 6th & Water St SW, DC	(202) 554-8000

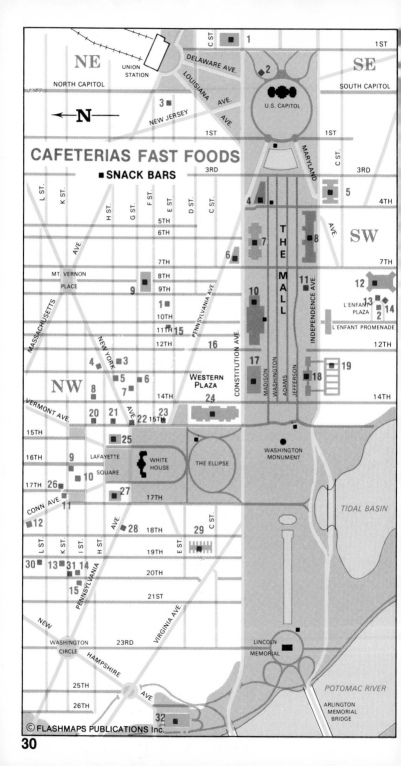

CAFETERIAS FAST FOODS

■ SNACK BARS

NE

SE

SW

NW

UNION STATION

U.S. CAPITOL

THE MALL

L'ENFANT PLAZA

L'ENFANT PROMENADE

WESTERN PLAZA

MT. VERNON PLACE

LAFAYETTE SQUARE

WHITE HOUSE

THE ELLIPSE

WASHINGTON MONUMENT

TIDAL BASIN

LINCOLN MEMORIAL

POTOMAC RIVER

ARLINGTON MEMORIAL BRIDGE

WASHINGTON CIRCLE

NORTH CAPITOL

SOUTH CAPITOL

DELAWARE AVE.

LOUISIANA AVE.

NEW JERSEY

MARYLAND AVE.

PENNSYLVANIA AVE.

CONSTITUTION AVE.

INDEPENDENCE AVE.

MASSACHUSETTS AVE.

NEW YORK AVE.

VERMONT AVE.

CONN. AVE.

NEW HAMPSHIRE

VIRGINIA AVE.

MADISON

WASHINGTON

ADAMS

JEFFERSON

← N →

© FLASHMAPS PUBLICATIONS Inc.

30

CAFETERIAS/CAFES—BY MAP NUMBERS

1 New Senate Office	12 Dept H.U.D.	23 Shops, The
2 Supreme Court	13 Greenhouse	24 Dept Commerce
3 Bellevue Hotel	14 Gourmet Too	25 Court Claims
4 Natl Gallery Art New	15 Kitcheteria	26 YWCA
5 Dept. H.E.W.	16 Pavilion-Old PO	27 New Executive
6 Fed Trade Comm.	17 Mus Amer History	28 All States
7 Natl Gallery Art	18 Dept Agriculture N	29 Dept Interior
8 Air & Space	19 Dept Agriculture S	30 Dutch Treat
9 National Portrait	20 Chamberlin's	31 China Grove
10 Mus Natural History	21 John's Frisco	31 Sholl's
11 Hirshhorn Cafe	22 Peoples	32 Encore

CAFETERIAS/CAFES—ALPHABETICAL

Cafeteria/Cafe	Address	Map No	Hours
Air & Space Museum	7th & Independence	8	10:00-5:00
All States	1750 Pennsylvania Ave NW	28	7:30-7:30
Bellevue Hotel	15 E St NW	3	7:00-8:00
Chamberlin's	819 15th St NW	20	7:30-2:30
China Grove	1990 K St NW	31	11:00-4:00
Court of Claims	717 Madison Pl NW	25	12:00-2:00
Dept of Agriculture-North	14th St & Independence	18	7:00-4:00
Dept of Agriculture-South	14th St & Independence	19	7:00-4:00
Dept of Commerce	14th St & Constitution	24	7:00-2:00
Department of H.E.W.	330 Independence SW	5	7:00-3:15
Department of H.U.D.	451 7th St SW	12	7:30-2:00
Dept of Interior	18th St & C NW	29	7:00-3:15
Dutch Treat Two	1901 L St NW	30	7:30-6:00
Encore Cafeteria	Kennedy Center	32	11:30-8:00
Federal Trade Commission	6th St & Pennsylvania NW	6	7:45-3:15
Gourmet Too	609 l'Enfant Plaza	14	7:00-4:00
Greenhouse, The Cafe	480 l'Enfant Plaza	13	7:00-3:00
Hirshhorn Outdoor Cafe	7th & Independence SW	11	May-Oct
John's Frisco	737 15th St NW	21	7:00-4:00
Kitcheteria	11th St & E NW	15	7:00-9:00
Museum of American History	12th & Constitution	17	11:00-8:00
Museum of Natural History	10th & Constitution	10	11:00-4:00
National Portrait Gallery	8th & 9th Sts NW	9	10:00-4:30
National Gallery of Art	6th & Constitution	7	11:00-3:30
National Gallery (New Wing)	4th & Constitution	4	11:00-4:30
New Executive Office Bldg	17th St & H NW	27	7:45-3:15
New Senate Office Bldg	1st St & Constitution	1	1:30-3:30
People's Cafeteria	15th & New York NW	22	7:00-7:00
Sholl's-Colonial	1990 K St NW	31	7:00-8:00
Supreme Court Cafeteria	1 First St NE	2	7:30-2:00
YWCA	1649 K St NW	21	7:15-2:15

The Pavilion · Old Post Office   1100 Pennsylvania Ave NW   16   10:00-9:30
CATSKILLS DELI, ENRICO'S, FETTUCINI, FRENCH FRYE, FLYING FRUIT, INDIAN DELIGHT, INTERNATIONAL DOGS, PANDA CAFE, PEDESTRIAN CAFE, TACO DON'S, TEXAS CATTLE, WINGMASTERS

The Shops   1331 Pennsylvania Ave   23   10:00-7:00
AU BON PAIN, BAGEL PLACE, BOARDWALK FRIES, BULL ON BEACH, EVERYTHING YOGURT, HUNAN EXPRESS, INCREDIBLE VEGETABLES, JERRY'S SUBS, MAMMA LLARDO'S PIZZA, ROY ROGERS, SONIA'S SWEETS, STUFT POTATOE

FAST FOOD—BY MAP NUMBERS

1 McDonald's	6 Wendy's	11 Blue Chip
2 Roy Rogers	7 Roy Rogers	12 McDonald's
3 Holly Farms	8 McDonald's	13 McDonald's
4 Roy Rogers	9 Burger King	14 Wendy's
5 German Deli	10 Hardees	15 Roy Rogers

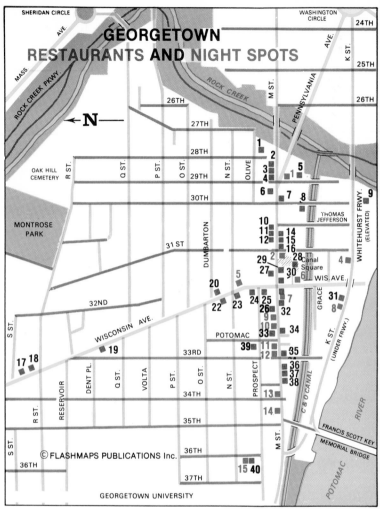

Night Spot	Address	Map No.	Type	Telephone
Annie's	3204 M St	7	Country/Blues	333-6767
Bayou, The	3135 K St NW	4	Rock/Dancing	333-2897
Blues Alley	1073 Wisconsin	6	Jazz/Blues	337-4141
Cellar Door, The	1204 34th St NW	13	Jazz/Folk/Blues	337-3389
Champions	1206 Wisconsin	5	DJ & Dancing	965-4005
Charlie's	3223 K St	8	Top Live Jazz	337-7100
Desiree	Four Seasons Htl	1	Disco/Dancing	342-0820
F. Scott's	1226 36th NW	15	DJ & Dancing	965-1789
J & B Crazy Horse	3259 M St NW	12	Live Rock	333-0400
Mr. Henry's G'town	1225 Wisconsin	5	Piano Bar	337-4334
Mr. Smith's	3104 M St NW	2	Jazz/Blues/Guitar	333-3104
Paul Mall	3235 M St NW	9	Rock/Dancing	965-5353
Poseur's	3403 M St NW	14	New Wave	965-5600
Saloon, The	3239 M St	10	Live Jazz	338-4900
Winston's	3295 M St NW	11	Disco	333-3150

GEORGETOWN RESTAURANTS—BY MAP NUMBERS

1 Hunan Garden	14 Daressalem	30 Nathan's
2 El Tio Pepe	15 Le Steak	31 Chadwick's
3 Enriqueta's	16 Apana	32 Houlihan's
4 La Chaumiere	17 La Nicoise	32 Samurai Japan
5 Aux Beaux Champs	18 Japan Inn	33 Fettoosh
6 Guards, The	20 Au Pied de Cochon	34 Clyde's
7 Vietnam G'town	22 G'town Bar/Grill	35 El Caribe
8 Foundry	23 Martin's Tavern	35 Las Pampas
9 Hisago	25 Third Edition	36 Tandoor
9 Potomac	26 Uno's Chicago	37 Bamiyan
10 Charing Cross	27 Mrs C.'s Chinoiserie	37 Madurai
11 Chez Grandmere	28 Cafe La Ruche	39 Morton's
12 J. Odette	29 Bistro Francais	40 1789

GEORGETOWN RESTAURANTS—ALPHABETICAL

Restaurant	Address	Map No.	Cuisine	Average Price ★	Telephone
Aux Beaux Champs	Four Seasons Hotel	5	French	$35 +	342-0810
Apana	3066 M St NW	16	Indian	30-40	965-3040
Au Pied de Cochon	1335 Wis NW	20	French	8-14	333-5440
Bamiyan	3320 M St NW	37	Afghan	8-12	338-1896
Bistro Francais	3128 M St NW	29	French	15-20	338-3830
Cafe La Ruche	1039 31st St NW	28	French	12-15	965-2684
Chadwick's G'town	3205 K St NW	31	American	8-12	333-2565
Charing Cross	3027 M St NW	10	Steak/Ale	10-15	338-2141
Chez Grand-mere	3057 M St NW	11	French	10-15	337-2436
Clyde's	3236 M St NW	34	American	10-15	333-0294
Daressalem	3056 M St NW	14	Moroccan	20-30	342-1925
El Caribe	3288 M St NW	35	Latin-Amer	10-15	338-3121
El Tio Pepe	2809 M St NW	2	Spanish	15-20	337-0730
Enriqueta's	2811 M St NW	3	Mexican	9-15	338-7772
Fettoosh	3277 M St NW	33	Lebanese	12-18	342-1199
Foundry, The	1050 30th St NW	8	American	12-20	337-1500
G'town Bar & Grill	1310 Wisconsin	22	American	20-25	337-7777
Guards, The	2915 M St NW	6	American	12-20	965-2350
Hisago	3050 K St NW	9	Japanese	40-50	944-4282
Houlihan's	3222 M St NW	32	American	10-15	342-2280
Hunan Garden	1201 28th St	1	Szechuan	10-14	965-6800
J. Odette	3063 M St NW	12	Italian	20-30	333-7038
Japan Inn	1715 Wisconsin	18	Japanese	15-20	337-3400
La Chaumiere	2813 M St NW	4	French	10-15	338-1784
La Nicoise	1721 Wisconsin	17	French	15-25	965-9300
Las Pampas	3291 M St NW	35	Argentinian	15-20	333-5151
Le Steak	3060 M St NW	15	Steak	15-20	965-1627
Madurai	3318 M St NW	37	Vegetarian	8-10	333-0997
Martin's Tavern	1264 Wisconsin	23	American	8-12	333-7370
Morton's of Chicago	3251 Prospect St	39	Beef/Lobster	35 +	342-6258
Mrs. C.'s Chinoiserie	3139 M St NW	27	Chinese	25 +	337-6100
Nathan's	3150 M St NW	30	No. Italian	20-25	338-2000
Potomac	30th & K St NW	9	Continental	18-30	944-4200
Samurai Japan Steak	3222 M St NW	32	Japanese	10-20	333-1001
1789, The	1226 36th St NW	40	French	35 +	965-1789
Tandoor	3316 M St NW	36	Indian	15-20	333-3376
Third Edition	1218 Wisconsin	25	American	8-14	333-3700
Uno's Chicago	3211 M St	26	Pizza	7-10	965-6333
Vietnam Georgetown	2934 M St	7	Vietnamese	10-15	337-4536

★ Prices do not include drinks or gratuities

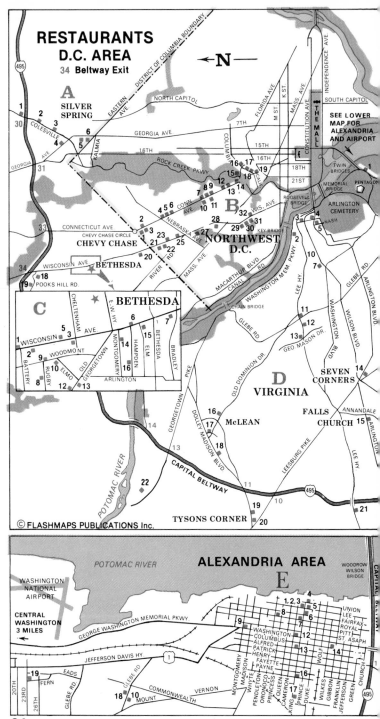

RESTAURANTS
D.C. AREA
34 Beltway Exit

←—N—→

DISTRICT OF COLUMBIA BOUNDARY

A
SILVER SPRING

SEE LOWER MAP FOR ALEXANDRIA AND AIRPORT

COLESVILLE
GEORGIA AVE
EASTERN AVE
NORTH CAPITOL
7TH
FLORIDA AVE
K ST
M ST
MASS. AVE
INDEPENDENCE AVE
SOUTH CAPITOL
CONSTITUTION AVE
THE MALL

KALMIA
16TH
15TH
COLUMBIA
ROCK CREEK PKWY
16TH
18TH
21ST
TWIN BRIDGES
MEMORIAL BRIDGE
PENTAGON

GEORGIA AVE

B
CONN. AVE
NEBRASKA AVE
WIS. AVE
ARLINGTON CEMETERY
NASH

CONNECTICUT AVE
CHEVY CHASE CIRCLE
CHEVY CHASE
Key Bridge
ROOSEVELT BRIDGE

NORTHWEST D.C.

BETHESDA
WISCONSIN AVE
POOKS HILL RD.
RIVER RD.
MASS. AVE
MACARTHUR BLVD
CANAL RD
CHAIN BRIDGE
WASHINGTON MEM. PKWY.
LEE HY.
GLEBE RD
GLEBE RD
WASHINGTON BLVD
ARLINGTON BLVD
WILSON BLVD

C
BETHESDA
E-W HY.
CHELTENHAM AVE
WISCONSIN
MONTGOMERY
WOODMONT
BATTERY
RUGBY
ELMO
OLD GEORGETOWN
ARLINGTON
HAMPDEN
ELM
BETHESDA
BRADLEY

GEORGETOWN PIKE
OLD DOMINION DR
DOLLEY MADISON BLVD
GEO. MASON DR.
LEESBURG PIKE
LEE HY.

D
VIRGINIA

SEVEN CORNERS

FALLS CHURCH
ANNANDALE
ARLINGTON

McLEAN

POTOMAC RIVER

CAPITAL BELTWAY

TYSONS CORNER

© FLASHMAPS PUBLICATIONS Inc.

POTOMAC RIVER

ALEXANDRIA AREA
WOODROW WILSON BRIDGE

E

WASHINGTON NATIONAL AIRPORT

CENTRAL WASHINGTON 3 MILES

GEORGE WASHINGTON MEMORIAL PKWY

JEFFERSON DAVIS HY.
EADS
FERN
GLEBE RD
COMMONWEALTH
MOUNT
VERNON
WASHINGTON
COLUMBUS
ALFRED
PATRICK
HENRY
FAYETTE
PAYNE
MONTGOMERY
MADISON
WHYTE
PENDLETON
ORONOCO
PRINCESS
QUEEN
CAMERON
KING
PRINCE
DUKE
WOLF
WILKES
GIBBON
FRANKLIN
JEFFERSON
GREEN
UNION
LEE
FAIRFAX
ROYAL
PITT
ST. ASAPH
CHURCH

20TH
23RD
26TH

34

RESTAURANTS—D.C. AREA

SILVER SPRING A-Area

Restaurant	Address	Map No.	Cuisine	Average Price ★	Area 301 Telephone
Crisfield	8012 Georgia	A5	Seafood	$15-20	589-1306
Fred & Harry's	10110 Colesville	A1	Seafood	12-20	593-7177
Mamma Regina	8727 Colesville	A3	Italian	12-18	585-1040
Mrs. K's Tollhouse	9201 Colesville	A2	American	10-15	589-3500
Sakura Palace	7926 Georgia	A6	Japanese	15-25	587-7070
Wellington's	8777 Georgia	A4	Seafood	10-15	587-4600

NORTHWEST DC B-Area

Area 202

Restaurant	Address	Map No.	Cuisine	Average Price ★	Telephone
Adriatico	4515 Wisconsin	B27	Italian	10-15	686-1882
Alfio's La Trattoria	5100 Wisconsin	B21	Italian	10-20	966-0091
Cafe Burgundy	5031 Conn Ave	B4	French	10-15	686-5300
Caffe Italiano	3516 Conn Ave	B11	Italian	9-15	966-2172
Calvert Restaurant	1967 Calvert	B15	Mid East	7-10	232-5431
Csiko's	3601 Conn Ave	B7	Hungarian	10-20	362-5624
Dancing Crab	4611 Wisconsin	B25	Seafood	12-18	244-1882
David Lee's Empress	1875 Conn Ave	B19	Chinese	9-14	462-8110
El Caribe	1828 Columbia	B17	Cuban	12-20	234-6969
Fishery, The	5511 Conn Ave	B2	Seafood	16-25	363-2144
Floriana	4936 Wisconsin	B22	Italian	10-15	362-9009
Germaine's	2400 Wisconsin	B31	Vietnamese	25-30	965-1185
Hunan Gallery	3308 Wisconsin	B28	Chinese	10-15	362-6645
Ivy's Place	3520 Conn Ave	B10	Thai/Indnsia	8-12	363-7802
La Fourchette	2429 18th St	B16	French	15-20	332-3077
L'Escargot	3309 Conn Ave	B9	French	12-20	966-7510
Le Caprice	2348 Wisconsin	B31	French	18-24	337-3394
Lotus Inn	2404 Wisconsin	B30	Chinese	8-15	337-8080
Malabar	4934 Wisconsin	B22	Indian	10-15	363-8900
Napoleon's	2649 Conn Ave	B13	French	15-20	265-8955
New Orleans Emprum	2477 18th St	B17	Cajun	15-20	328-3421
Old Europe	2434 Wisconsin	B29	German	15-20	333-7600
Omega	1856 Columbia	B18	Cuban	8-12	745-9158
Peking	5522 Conn Ave	B1	Chinese	7-12	966-8079
Petitto's	2653 Conn Ave	N12	Italian	10-18	667-5350
Piccadilly	5510 Conn Ave	B3	English	15-20	966-7600
Pleasant Peasant	5300 Wisconsin	B20	American	20-25	364-2500
Red Sea	2463 18th St NW	B16	Ethiopian	8-12	483-5000
Roma	3419 Conn Ave	B8	Italian	12-16	363-6611
Round Table	4859 Wisconsin	B23	Internat'l	9-14	362-1250
Shanghai Garden	4469 Conn Ave	B6	Chinese	7-12	362-3000
Sushi-Ko	2309 Wisconsin	B32	Japanese	10-15	333-4187
Thai Room	5037 Conn Ave	B5	Thai	9-15	244-5933
Tucson Cantina	2605 Conn Ave	B14	Mexican	8-10	462-6410
Viet Chateau	2637 Conn Ave	B12	Vietnamese	9-15	232-6464
Yenching Palace	3524 Conn Ave	B10	Chinese	10-15	362-8200

BETHESDA C-Area

Area 301

Restaurant	Address	Map No.	Cuisine	Average Price ★	Telephone
Benihana of Tokyo	7315 Wisconsin	C6	Japanese	10-15	652-5391
Bernie's	5400 Pooks Hill	C19	American	9-14	530-0300
Bish Thompson's	7935 Wisconsin	C12	Seafood	12-20	656-2400
China Coral	6900 Wisconsin	C7	Chinese	12-14	656-1203
China Garden	4711 Montgomery	C14	Chinese	10-15	657-4665
Flaps Up	4723 Elm St	C15	American	10-16	654-1530
Frascati	4806 Rugby	C8	Italian	10-14	652-9514

★ Prices do not include drinks or gratuities

Restaurant	Address	Map No	Cuisine	Price ★	Telephone
Kaori Hana	7944 Wisconsin	C5	Japanese	$10-18	951-8771
Michel's	7904 Woodmont	C10	French	10-14	656-0720
Nara	7756 Wisconsin	C5	Japanese	12-15	986-9696
North China	7814 Old G'town	C13	Chinese	10-15	656-7922
O'Donnell's Sea Grill	8301 Wisconsin	C1	Seafood	10-15	656-6200
Peppermill	8120 Wisconsin	C2	French	10-15	652-2000
Pines of Rome	4709 Hampden	C16	Italian	10-15	657-8775
Raleigh Inn	8011 Woodmont	C9	American	10-15	652-4244
Szechuan Garden	7800 Wisconsin	C3	Chinese	8-12	652-1700
Vagabond	7315 Wisconsin	C6	Centrl Eurp	15-20	654-2575

VIRGINIA D-Area
Area 703

Restaurant	Address	Map No	Cuisine	Price	Telephone
Alpine	4770 Lee Hwy	D12	Italian	10-15	528-7600
Casa Maria	Rte123-Tysons	D19	Mexican	10-15	893-2443
Chalet de la Paix	4506 Lee Hwy	D11	European	20+	522-6777
Charlie's Place	6930 Old Dom Dr	D16	American	9-14	893-1034
Company Inkwell	8240 Leesbrg Pike	D20	French	35+	356-0300
Evans Farm Inn	1696 Chain Brdg	D18	American	15-20	356-8000
Hsian Foong	1836 Wilson Blvd	D10	Chinese	10-15	528-8886
Inn Eight Immortals	7 Corners Center	D14	Chinese	10-15	534-3043
Kazan's	6813 Redmond	D17	Mid East	10-20	734-1960
La Guinguette	8111 Lee Hwy	D21	French	25-30	560-3220
L'Alouette	2045 Wilson Blvd	D7	French	15-20	525-1750
L'Auberge Chez Fran.	332 Springvale Rd	D22	Alsatian	19-21	759-3800
Little Europe	3018 Annandale	D15	Hungarian	8-15	241-5580
Orleans House	1213 Wilson Blvd	D3	American	10-15	524-2929
S & S Livestock	Marriott Tw Brdg	D1	Steak	12-15	628-4200
Shanghai	5157 Lee Hwy	D13	Chinese	6-14	536-7446
Top o' the Town	14th & N Oak	D5	American	25+	525-9200
Windows	1000 Wilson Blvd	D4	California	25-30	527-4430
View, The	Marriott-Key Brdg	D2	Continental	20-30	524-6400

ALEXANDRIA & AIRPORT E-Area
Area 703

Restaurant	Address	Map No	Cuisine	Price	Telephone
Chez Andre	10 E Glebe St	E18	French	35+	836-1404
Chez Froggy	509 S 23rd St	E10	French	12-16	979-7676
China Gate	310 N Fairfax	E8	Chinese	10-15	548-8080
Fish Market	105 King Street	E2	Seafood	10-15	836-5676
Gadsby's Tavern	138 N Royal St	E7	American	10-15	548-1288
Geno's	1300 King Street	E16	Ital/Amer	10-14	549-1796
Geranio	722 King Street	E17	Italian	10-15	548-0088
Hamiltons	214 King Street	E6	Seafood	10-15	683-6868
Il Porto	121 King Street	E1	Italian	10-20	836-8833
Kristos Charcoal Hse	608 Montgomery	E9	Beef	12-15	683-9864
La Bergerie	218 N Lee Street	D10	French	25+	683-1007
Landini Brothers	115 King Street	E2	Ital/Seafd	12-18	836-8404
Le Chardon d'Or	116 S Alfred St	E13	Lt French	45-65	838-8008
Le Refuge	127 N Washingtn	E12	French	14-18	548-4661
Old Club	555 S Washington	E14	Southern	9-14	549-4555
Portofino	526 S 23rd St	E19	Italian	25-35	979-8200
Seaport Inn, The	6 King Street	E4	Stk/Seafd	12-18	549-2341
Taverna Cretekou	818 King Street	E13	Greek	8-12	548-8688
Terrazza	710 King Street	E12	Italian	25-35	683-6900
Two-Nineteen	219 King Street	E7	Fr Creole	15-25	549-1141
Wayfarer	110 S Pitt Street	E6	English	12-25	836-2749
Wharf, The	119 King Street	E3	Seafood	15-19	836-2834

★ *Prices do not include drinks or gratuities*

THE WHITE HOUSE

Second Floor

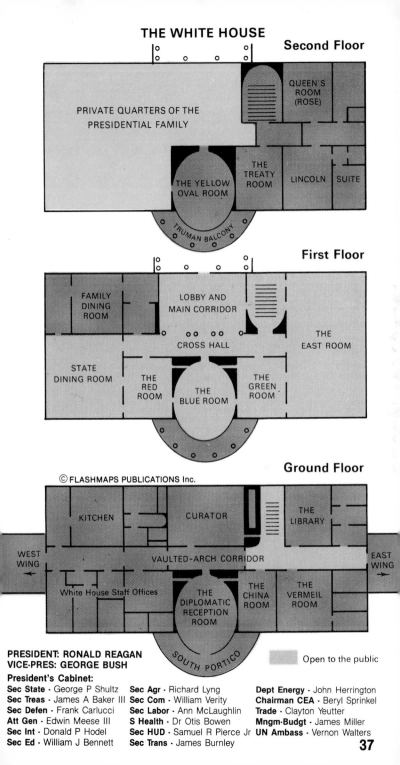

PRIVATE QUARTERS OF THE
PRESIDENTIAL FAMILY

QUEEN'S
ROOM
(ROSE)

THE
YELLOW
OVAL ROOM

THE
TREATY
ROOM

LINCOLN · SUITE

TRUMAN BALCONY

First Floor

FAMILY
DINING
ROOM

LOBBY AND
MAIN CORRIDOR

THE
EAST ROOM

CROSS HALL

STATE
DINING ROOM

THE
RED
ROOM

THE
BLUE ROOM

THE
GREEN
ROOM

© FLASHMAPS PUBLICATIONS Inc.

Ground Floor

KITCHEN

CURATOR

THE
LIBRARY

WEST
WING

VAULTED-ARCH CORRIDOR

EAST
WING

White House Staff Offices

THE
DIPLOMATIC
RECEPTION
ROOM

THE
CHINA
ROOM

THE
VERMEIL
ROOM

SOUTH PORTICO

Open to the public

PRESIDENT: RONALD REAGAN
VICE-PRES: GEORGE BUSH

President's Cabinet:

Sec State · George P Shultz	**Sec Agr** · Richard Lyng	**Dept Energy** · John Herrington
Sec Treas · James A Baker III	**Sec Com** · William Verity	**Chairman CEA** · Beryl Sprinkel
Sec Defen · Frank Carlucci	**Sec Labor** · Ann McLaughlin	**Trade** · Clayton Yeutter
Att Gen · Edwin Meese III	**S Health** · Dr Otis Bowen	**Mngm·Budgt** · James Miller
Sec Int · Donald P Hodel	**Sec HUD** · Samuel R Pierce Jr	**UN Ambass** · Vernon Walters
Sec Ed · William J Bennett	**Sec Trans** · James Burnley	

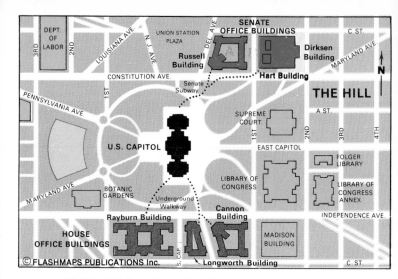

THE ONE—HUNDREDTH CONGRESS

THE SENATE
Vice-President : George Bush
Pres. Pro Temp : John Stennis
Majority Leader : Robert Byrd
Majority Whip : Alan Cranston
Minority Leader : Robert Dole
Minority Whip : Alan K. Simpson

HOUSE OF REPRESENTATIVES
Speaker : Jim Wright
Majority Leader : Thomas S. Foley
Majority Whip : Tony Coelho
Minority Leader : Robert H. Michel
Minority Whip : Trent Lott

SENATE AND HOUSE Terms end January 3rd
SENATE TERM : 6 Years   **HOUSE TERM : 2 Years**
Names in Blue   Names in Black

CONGRESSIONAL DIRECTORY—BY STATE
Congressional Telephone Number: (202) 224-3121

ALABAMA
Heflin, Howell (D)	Term - 1991
Shelby, Richard C. (D)	Term: 1993
Bevill, Tom (D)	4th District
Callahan, H. L. (R)	1st District
Dickinson, William (R)	2nd District
Erdreich, Ben (D)	6th District
Flippo, Ronnie G (D)	5th District
Harris, Claude (D)	7th District
Nichols, Bill (D)	3rd District

ALASKA
Murkowski, Frank (R)	Term - 1993
Stevens, Ted (R)	Term - 1991
Young, Donald E. (R)	At Large

ARIZONA
De Concini, Dennis (D)	Term - 1989
McCain, John (R)	Term - 1993
Rhodes, John III (R)	1st District
Kolbe, Jim (R)	5th District
Kyl, Jon (R)	4th District
Stump, Bob (D)	3rd District
Udall, Morris K (D)	2nd District

ARKANSAS
Bumpers, Dale (D)	Term - 1993
Pryor, David H (D)	Term - 1989
Alexander, Bill (D)	1st District
Anthony, Beryl, Jr. (D)	4th District
Hammerschmidt, J (R)	3rd District
Robinson, Tommy (D)	2nd District

CALIFORNIA

Cranston, Alan (D)	Term - 1993
Wilson, Pete (R)	Term - 1989
Anderson, Glenn M. (D)	32nd District
Badham, Robert E. (R)	40th District
Bates, Jim (D)	44th District
Bellenson, Anthony (D)	23rd District
Berman, Howard L (D)	26th District
Bosco, Douglas H. (D)	1st District
Boxer, Barbara (D)	6th District
Brown, George E. (D)	36th District
Burton, Sala (D)	5th District
Coelho, Tony (D)	15th District
Dannemeyer, Wm (R)	39th District
Dellums, Ronald V. (D)	8th District
Dixon, Julian (D)	28th District
Dornan, Robert K (R)	38th District
Drier, Dave (R)	33rd District
Dymally, Mervyn (D)	31st District
Edwards, Don (D)	10th District
Fazio, Vic (D)	4th District
Gallegly, Elton (R)	21st District
Hawkins, Augustus (D)	29th District
Herger, Wally (R)	2nd District
Hunter, Duncan (R)	45th District
Konnyu, E (R)	12th District
Lagomarsino, Robt. (R)	19th District
Lantos, Tom (D)	11th District
Lehman, Richard (D)	18th District
Levine, Mel (D)	27th District
Lewis, Jerry (R)	35th District
Lowery, Bill (R)	41st District
Lungren, Dan E. (R)	42nd District
Martinez, Matthew (D)	30th District
Matsui, Robert (D)	3rd District
McCandless, Al (R)	37th District
Miller, George (D)	7th District
Mineta, Norman (D)	13th District
Moorhead, Carlos (R)	22nd District
Packard, Ronald (R)	43rd District
Panetta, Leon (D)	16th District
Pashayan, Charles (R)	17th District
Roybal, Edward R. (D)	25th District
Shumway, Norman (R)	14th District
Stark, Fortney (D)	9th District
Thomas, William (R)	20th District
Torres, Esteban (D)	34th District
Waxman, Henry (D)	24th District

COLORADO

Armstrong, William (R)	Term - 1991
Wirth, Timothy E (D)	Term - 1993
Brown, Hank (R)	4th District
Hefley, Joel (R)	5th District
Campbell, Ben (D)	3rd District
Schaefer, D. L.(R)	6th District
Schroeder, Patricia (D)	1st District
Skaggs, David (D)	2nd District

CONNECTICUT

Dodd, Christopher J.	Term - 1993
Weicker, Lowell, Jr. (R)	Term - 1989
Gejdenson, Sam (D)	2nd District
Johnson, Nancy L (R)	6th District
Kennelly, Barbara B (D)	1st District
McKinney, Stewart (R)	4th District
Morrison, Bruce (D)	3rd District
Rowland, John G (R)	5th District

DELAWARE

Biden, Joseph Jr. (D)	Term - 1991
Roth, William V. Jr. (R)	Term - 1989
Carper, Thomas R (D)	At Large

DISTRICT OF COLUMBIA
Fauntroy, Walter E (D)

FLORIDA

Chiles, Lawton (D)	Term - 1991
Graham, Bob (D)	Term - 1993
Bennett, Charles E. (D)	3rd District
Bilirakis, Michael (R)	9th District
Chappell, Bill Jr. (D)	4th District
Fascell, Dante B. (D)	19th District
Gibbons, Sam (D)	7th District
Grant, Bill (D)	2nd District
Hutto, Earl (D)	1st District
Ireland, Andy (D)	10th District
Lehman, William (D)	17th District
Lewis, Tom (R)	12th District
MacKay, Buddy (D)	6th District
Mack, Connie (R)	13th District
McCollum, Bill (R)	5th District
Mica, Don (D)	14th District
Nelson, Bill (D)	11th District
Pepper, Claude (D)	18th District
Shaw, E Clay, Jr. (R)	15th District
Smith, Larry (D)	16th District
Young, C. W. (R)	8th District

Congressional Telephone Number: (202) 224-3121

GEORGIA

Nunn, Sam (D)	Term - 1991
Fowler, Wyche Jr (D)	Term - 1993
Barnard, Doug, Jr. (D)	10th District
Darden, George (D)	7th District
Gingrich, Newt (R)	6th District
Hatcher, Charles (D)	2nd District
Jenkins, Ed (D)	9th District
Lewis, John (D)	5th District
Ray, Richard (D)	3rd District
Rowland, J Roy (D)	8th District
Swindall, Pat (R)	4th District
Thomas, Lindsay (D)	1st District

HAWAII

Inouye, Daniel K. (D)	Term - 1993
Matsunaga, Spark (D)	Term - 1989
Akaka, Daniel K. (D)	2nd District
Saiki, Patricia (R)	1st District

IDAHO

McClure, James (R)	Term - 1991
Symms, Steven D. (R)	Term - 1993
Craig, Larry (R)	1st District
Stallings, Rich (D)	2nd District

ILLINOIS

Dixon, Alan J. (D)	Term - 1993
Simon, Paul (D)	Term - 1991
Annunzio, Frank (D)	11th District
Bruce, Terry (D)	19th District
Collins, Cardiss (D)	7th District
Crane, Philip M. (R)	12th District
Davis, Jack (R)	4th District
Durbin, Richard J (D)	20th District
Evans, Lane (D)	17th District
Fawell, Harris W. (R)	13th District
Gray, Kenneth J (D)	22nd District
Hastert, Dennis (R)	14th District
Hayes, Charles A (D)	1st District
Hyde, Henry J. (R)	6th District
Lipinski, William (D)	5th District
Madigan, Edward R. (R)	15th District
Martin, Lynn (R)	16th District
Michel, Robert H. (R)	18th District
Porter, John (R)	10th District
Price, Melvin (D)	21st District
Rostenkowski, Dan (D)	8th District
Russo, Martin (D)	3rd District
Savage, Gus (D)	2nd District
Yates, Sidney R. (D)	9th District

INDIANA

Lugar, Richard G. (R)	Term - 1989
Quayle, Dan (R)	Term - 1993
Burton, Dan (R)	6th District
Coats, Dan (R)	4th District
Hamilton, Lee H. (D)	9th District
Hiler, John (R)	3rd District
Jacobs, Andrew, Jr. (D)	10th District
Jontz, James (D)	5th District
McCloskey, Frank (D)	8th District
Myers, John T. (R)	7th District
Sharp, Philip R. (D)	2nd District
Visclosky, Peter (D)	1st District

IOWA

Grassley, Charles E. (R)	Term - 1993
Harkin, Tom (D)	Term - 1991
Grandy, Fred (R)	6th District
Leach, James A.S. (R)	1st District
Lightfoot, J R (R)	5th District
Nagle, David (D)	3rd District
Smith, Neal (D)	4th District
Tauke, Thomas (R)	2nd District

KANSAS

Dole, Robert (R)	Term - 1993
Kassebaum, Nancy (R)	Term - 1991
Glickman, Dan (D)	4th District
Meyers , Jan (R)	3rd District
Roberts, Pat (R)	1st District
Slattery, Jim (D)	2nd District
Whittaker, Robert (R)	5th District

KENTUCKY

Ford, Wendell, H. (D)	Term - 1993
McConnell, A. M. (R)	Term - 1991
Bunning, Jim (R)	4th District
Hopkins, Larry (R)	6th District
Hubbard, Carroll, Jr. (D)	1st District
Mazzoli, Romano L. (D)	3rd District
Natcher, William H. (D)	2nd District
Perkins, Carl D. (D)	7th District
Rogers, Harold (R)	5th District

LOUISIANA

Johnston, J. Bennett (D)	Term - 1991
Breaux, John B. (D)	Term 1993
Boggs, Lindy Hill (D)	2nd District
Baker, Richard (R)	6th District
Hayes, James (D)	7th District
Holloway, Clyde C (R)	8th District

Huckaby, Jerry (D)	5th District
Livingston, Bob (R)	1st District
Roemer, Charles (D)	4th District
Tauzin, Billy (D)	3rd District

MAINE

Cohen, William S. (R)	Term - 1991
Mitchell, George (D)	Term - 1989
Brennan, Joseph (D)	1st District
Snowe, Olympia (R)	2nd District

MARYLAND

Sarbanes, Paul S. (D)	Term - 1989
Mikulski, Barbara (D)	Term - 1993
Bentley, H. Delich (R)	2nd District
Byron, Beverly B. (D)	6th District
Cardin, Benjamin (D)	3rd District
Dyson, Royden (D)	1st District
Hoyer, Stenyh (D)	5th District
McMillen, Tom (D)	4th District
Mfume, Kweisi (D)	7th District
Morella, Constance (R)	8th District

MASSACHUSETTS

Kennedy, Edw M. (D)	Term - 1989
Kerry, John (D)	Term - 1991
Atkins, Chester G. (D)	5th District
Boland, Edward M. (D)	2nd District
Conte, Silvio O. (R)	1st District
Donnelly, Brian (D)	11th District
Early, Joseph (D)	3rd District
Frank, Barney (D)	4th District
Kennedy, Joseph (D)	8th District
Markey, Edward J. (D)	7th District
Mavroules, Nicholas (D)	6th District
Moakley, Joe (D)	9th District
Studds, Gerry E. (D)	10th District

MICHIGAN

Levin, Carl M. (D)	Term - 1991
Riegle, Donald W. (D)	Term - 1989
Bonior, David E. (D)	12th District
Broomfield, Wm S (R)	18th District
Carr, Bob (D)	6th District
Conyers, John Jr. (D)	1st District
Crockett, George (D)	13th District
Davis, Robert (R)	11th District
Dingell, John D. (D)	16th District
Ford, William D. (D)	15th District
Henry, Paul B. (R)	5th District

Hertel, Dennis (D)	14th District
Jagt Vander, Guy (R)	9th District
Kildee, Dale E. (D)	7th District
Levin, Sander (D)	17th District
Pursell, Carl D (R)	2nd District
Schuette, Bill (R)	10th District
Traxler, Bob (D)	8th District
Upton, Fred (R)	4th District
Wolpe, Howard (D)	3rd District

MINNESOTA

Boschwitz, Rudy (R)	Term - 1989
Durenberger, David (R)	Term - 1993
Frenzel, Bill (R)	3rd District
Oberstar, James L (D)	8th District
Penny, Timothy J (D)	1st District
Sabo, Martin (D)	5th District
Sikorski, Gerry (D)	6th District
Stangeland, Arlen (R)	7th District
Vento, Bruce F. (D)	4th District
Weber, Vin (R)	2nd District

MISSISSIPPI

Cochran, Thad (R)	Term - 1991
Stennis, John C. (D)	Term - 1993
Dowdy, Wayne (D)	4th District
Espy, Michael (D)	2nd District
Lott, Trent (R)	5th District
Montgomery, G.V. (D)	3rd District
Whitten, Jamie L. (D)	1st District

MISSOURI

Danforth, John C. (R)	Term - 1989
Bond, Christopher (R)	Term - 1993
Bolling, Richard (D)	5th District
Buechner, Jack (R)	2nd District
Clay, William (Bill) (D)	1st District
Coleman, Thomas (R)	6th District
Emerson, Bill (R)	8th District
Gephardt, Richard (D)	3rd District
Skelton, Ike (D)	4th District
Taylor, Gene (R)	7th District
Volkmer, Harold L. (D)	9th District
Wheat, Alan (D)	5th District

MONTANA

Baucus, Max (D)	Term - 1991
Melcher, John (D)	Term - 1989
Marlenee, Ron (R)	2nd District
Williams, Pat (D)	1st District

NEBRASKA

Exon, James J. (D)	Term - 1991
Zorinsky, Edward (D)	Term - 1989
Bereuter, Douglas (R)	1st District
Daub, Hal (R)	2nd District
Smith, Virginia (R)	3rd District

NEVADA

Hecht, Charles (R)	Term - 1989
Reid, Harry (D)	Term - 1993
Bilbray, James (D)	1st District
Vucanovich, Barbara (R)	2nd District

NEW HAMPSHIRE

Humphrey, Gordon (R)	Term - 1989
Rudman, Warren (R)	Term - 1993
Gregg, Judd (R)	2nd District
Smith, Robert C. (R)	1st District

NEW JERSEY

Bradley, Bill (D)	Term - 1991
Lautenberg, Frank (D)	Term - 1989
Courter, Jim (R)	12th District
Dwyer, Bernard (D)	6th District
Florio, James J. (D)	1st District
Gallo, Dean A. (R)	11th District
Guarini, Frank J. (D)	14th District
Howard, James J. (D)	3rd District
Hughes, William J. (D)	2nd District
Rinaldo, Matthew J. (R)	7th District
Rodino, Peter, Jr. (D)	10th District
Roe, Robert A. (D)	8th District
Roukema, Marge (R)	5th District
Saxton, James H. (R)	13th District
Smith, Christopher (R)	4th District
Torricelli, Robert (D)	9th District

NEW MEXICO

Bingaman, Jeff (D)	Term - 1989
Domenici, Pete V. (R)	Term - 1993
Lujan, Manuel, Jr. (R)	1st District
Richardson, Bill (D)	3rd District
Skeen, Joseph R. (R)	2nd District

NEW YORK

Moynihan, Daniel P (D)	Term - 1989
D'Amato, Alfonse M (R)	Term - 1993
Ackerman, Gary (D)	7th District
Biaggi, Mario (D)	19th District
Boehlert, Sherwood (R)	25th District
DioGuardi, Joseph (R)	20th District
Downey, Thomas J. (D)	2nd District

NEW YORK Continued

Fish, Hamilton, Jr. (R)	21st District
Flake, Floyd (D)	6th District
Garcia, Robert (D)	18th District
Gilman, Benjamin (R)	22nd District
Green, S. Wm. (R)	15th District
Hochbrueckner G. (D)	1st District
Horton, Frank (R)	29th District
Houghton, Amory (R)	34th District
Kemp, Jack F. (R)	31st District
La Falce, John J. (D)	32nd District
Lent, Norman F. (R)	4th District
Manton, Thomas J (D)	9th District
Martin, David (R)	26th District
McGrath, R. J (R)	5th District
McHugh, Matthew (D)	28th District
Molinari, Guy (R)	14th District
Mrazek, Robert J (D)	3rd District
Nowak, Henry J. (D)	33rd District
Owens, Major R (D)	12th District
Rangel, Charles B. (D)	16th District
Scheuer, James H. (D)	8th District
Schumer, Charles (D)	10th District
Slaughter, Louise (D)	30th District
Solarz, Stephen J. (D)	13th District
Solomon, Gerald (R)	24th District
Stratton, Samuel S. (D)	23rd District
Towns, Edolphus (D)	11th District
Weiss, Theodore S. (D)	17th District
Wortley, George (R)	27th District

NORTH CAROLINA

Helms, Jesse A. (R)	Term - 1991
Sanford, Terry (D)	Term - 1993
Ballenger, Cass (R)	10th District
Coble, Howard (R)	6th District
Clark, Jaime (D)	11th District
Hefner, W.G. (Bill) (D)	8th District
Jones, Walter B. (D)	1st District
Lancaster, Martin (D)	3rd District
McMillan, Alex (R)	9th District
Neal, Stephen L. (D)	5th District
Price, David (D)	4th District
Rose, Charles III (D)	7th District
Valentine, I. Tim (D)	2nd District

NORTH DAKOTA

Burdick, Quentin N. (D)	Term - 1989
Conrad, Kent (D)	Term - 1993
Dorgan, Byron (D)	At Large

OHIO

Glenn, John (D)	Term - 1993
Metzenbaum, H. (D)	Term - 1989
Applegate, Douglas (D)	18th District
De Wine, Michael (R)	7th District
Eckart, Dennis (D)	11th District
Feighan, Edward F (D)	19th District
Gradison, Willis, Jr. (R)	2nd District
Hall, Tony P. (D)	3rd District
Kaptur, Marcy (D)	9th District
Kasich, John R (R)	12th District
Latta, Delbert L (R)	5th District
Luken, Thomas A (D)	1st District
Lukens, Donald E (R)	8th District
McEwen, Bob (R)	6th District
Miller, Clarence E. (R)	10th District
Oakar, Mary Rose (D)	20th District
Oxley, Michael G (R)	4th District
Pease, Donald J. (D)	13th District
Regula, Ralph S. (R)	16th District
Sawyer, Thomas (D)	14th District
Stokes, Louis (D)	21st District
Traficant, J. A., Jr. (R)	17th District
Wylie, Chalmers P. (R)	15th District

OKLAHOMA

Boren, David (D)	Term - 1991
Nickles, Don (R)	Term - 1993
Edwards, Mickey (R)	5th District
English, Glenn (D)	6th District
Inhofe, James (R)	1st District
McCurdy, David (D)	4th District
Synar, Mike (D)	2nd District
Watkins, Wes (D)	3rd District

OREGON

Hatfield, Mark O. (R)	Term - 1991
Packwood, Bob (R)	Term - 1993
AuCoin, Les (D)	1st District
DeFazio, Peter (D)	4th District
Smith, Denny (R)	5th District
Smith, Robert (R)	2nd District
Wyden, Ron (D)	3rd District

PENNSYLVANIA

Heinz, H. John III (R)	Term - 1989
Specter, Arlen (R)	Term - 1993
Borski, Robert A (D)	3rd District
Clinger, William Jr. (R)	23rd District
Coughlin, Lawrence (R)	13th District

PENNSYLVANIA Continued

Coyne, William (D)	14th District
Foglietta, Thomas (D)	1st District
Gaydos, Joseph M. (D)	20th District
Gekas, George W. (R)	17th District
Goodling, William F (R)	19th District
Gray, William H. III (D)	2nd District
Kanjorski, Paul E (D)	11th District
Kolter, Joseph P. (D)	4th District
Kosmayer, Peter H (D)	8th District
McDade, Joseph M (R)	10th District
Murphy, Austin J. (D)	22nd District
Murtha, John P. (D)	12th District
Ridge, Thomas J. (R)	21st District
Ritter, Donald (R)	15th District
Schulze, Richard T. (R)	5th District
Shuster, Bud (R)	9th District
Walgren, Doug (D)	18th District
Walker, Robert S. (R)	16th District
Weldon, Curt (R)	7th District
Yatron, Gus (D)	6th District

RHODE ISLAND

Chafee, John H. (R)	Term - 1989
Pell, Claiborne, (D)	Term - 1991
St. Germain, Fernand (D)	1st District
Schneider, C. (R)	2nd District

SOUTH CAROLINA

Hollings, Ernest F. (D)	Term - 1993
Thurmond, Strom (R)	Term - 1991
Derrick, Butler (D)	3rd District
Patterson, Elizabeth (D)	4th District
Ravenel, Arthur (R)	1st District
Spence, Floyd (R)	2nd District
Spratt, John (D)	5th District
Tallon, Robin (D)	6th District

SOUTH DAKOTA

Pressler, Larry (R)	Term 1991
Daschle, Thomas (D)	Term 1993
Johnson, Timothy (D)	At Large

TENNESSEE

Gore Jr, Albert (D)	Term - 1991
Sasser, James R. (D)	Term - 1989
Boner, William (D)	5th District
Cooper, James (D)	4th District
Duncan, John J. (R)	2nd District
Ford, Harold E. (D)	9th District
Gordon, Bart (D)	6th District

TENNESSEE Continued

Jones, Ed (D)	8th District
Lloyd, Marilyn (D)	3rd District
Quillen, James H. (R)	1st District
Sundquist, Don (R)	7th District

TEXAS

Bentsen, Lloyd (D)	Term - 1989
Gramm, Phil (R)	Term - 1991
Andrews, Mike (D)	25th District
Archer, Bill (R)	7th District
Armey, Richard (R)	26th District
Bartlett, Steve (R)	3rd District
Barton, Joe (R)	6th District
Boulter, Beau (R)	13th District
Brooks, Jack (D)	9th District
Bryant, John (D)	5th District
Bustamente, A. G. (D)	23rd District
Chapman, Jim (D)	1st District
Coleman, Ronald (D)	16th District
Combest, Larry (R)	19th District
de la Garza, E. (D)	15th District
DeLay, Tom (R)	22nd District
Fields, Jack (R)	8th District
Frost, Martin (D)	24th District
Gonzalez, Henry B (D)	20th District
Hall, Ralph (D)	4th District
Leath, Marvin (D)	11th District
Leland, Mickey (D)	18th District
Ortiz, Solomon P (D)	27th District
Pickle, J. J. (D)	10th District
Smith Lamar (R)	21st District
Stenholm, Charles (D)	17th District
Sweeney, Mac (R)	14th District
Wilson, Charles (D)	2nd District
Wright, Jim (D)	12th District

UTAH

Garn, Jake (R)	Term - 1993
Hatch, Orrin G. (R)	Term - 1989
Hansen, James (R)	1st District
Neilson, Howard C (R)	3rd District
Owens, Wayne (D)	2nd District

VERMONT

Leahy, Patrick J. (D)	Term - 1993
Stafford, Robert T. (R)	Term - 1989
Jeffords, James M. (R)	At Large

VIRGINIA

Trible, Paul S. Jr. (R)	Term - 1989
Warner, John W. (R)	Term - 1991
Bateman, Herbert H. (R)	1st District
Bliley, Thomas (R)	3rd District
Boucher, Frederick C (D)	9th District
Daniel, W. C. (Dan) (D)	5th District
Olin, James R (D)	6th District
Parris, Stanford (R)	8th District
Pickett, Owen (D)	2nd District
Sisisky, Norman (D)	4th District
Slaughter, D French (R)	7th District
Wolf, Frank (R)	10th District

WASHINGTON

Evans, Daniel J. (R)	Term - 1989
Adams, Brock (D)	Term - 1993
Bonker, Don (D)	3rd District
Chandler, Rod (R)	8th District
Dicks, Norman D. (D)	6th District
Foley, Thomas S. (D)	5th District
Lowry, Michael (D)	7th District
Miller, John (R)	1st District
Morrison, Sid (R)	4th District
Swift, Al (D)	2nd District

WEST VIRGINIA

Byrd, Robert C. (D)	Term - 1989
Rockefeller, J D IV (D)	Term - 1991
Mollohan, Alan B (D)	1st District
Rahall, Nick Joe II (D)	4th District
Staggers, Harley O Jr (D)	2nd District
Wise Jr, Robert (D)	3rd District

WISCONSIN

Kasten, Robert W. Jr. (R)	Term - 1993
Proxmire, William (D)	Term - 1989
Aspin, Les (D)	1st District
Gunderson, S. (R)	3rd District
Kastenmeier, Robert (D)	2nd District
Kleczka, Gerald D. (D)	4th District
Moody, James (D)	5th District
Obey, David R (D)	7th District
Petri, Thomas (R)	6th District
Roth, Tobias (R)	8th District
Sensenbrenner, Jas (R)	9th District

WYOMING

Simpson, Alan K. (R)	Term - 1991
Wallop, Malcolm (R)	Term - 1989
Cheney, Richard (R)	At Large

THE CAPITOL
Second Floor Plan

The Senate

1 Official Reporters of Debates
2 President's Room
3 The Marble Room
4 Formal Office of the Vice President
5 Reception Room
6 Office of the Vice President
7 Bill Clerk and Journal Clerk
8 Senators' Private Lobby
9 Chief Clerk
10 Secretary
11 Cloakrooms
12 Grand Staircase
13 Senate Majority Leader's Office
14 Senate Conference Room
15 Senate Minority Leader's Office
16 Executive Clerk
17-22 Senators' Private Offices
23 Senate Disbursing Office
24 Small Senate Rotunda
25 Senate Minority Whip
26-31 Senators' Private Offices

EAST FRONT

© FLASHMAPS PUBLICATIONS Inc.

The House

32 House Minority Leader's Office
33 Prayer Room
34 Representative's Private Office
35 House Majority Conference Room
36 House Minority Conference Room
37 House Subcommittee on Foreign Affairs
38 Congressional Ladies Reading Room
39 House Document Room
40 Office of the Speaker
41 House Reception Room
42 House Minority Whip
43 Committee on Ways and Means
44 Grand Staircase
45 Cloakrooms
46 Committee on Appropriations
47 Library
48 Members' Reading Rooms
49 Parliamentarian
50 Formal Office of the Speaker

■ Open to the Public

Two flags fly 24 hours a day over East and West Front (central part)

Tholus (top of dome) has lights that indicate if either house is sitting.

Flags that indicate which house is in session fly over wing of house in session.

The Supreme Court Justices: William H. Rhenquist, Chief Justice

William J. Brennan, Jr. Harry A. Blackmun Sandra Day O'Connor
Byron R. White Lewis F. Powell, Jr Antonin Scalia
Thurgood Marshall John P. Stevens

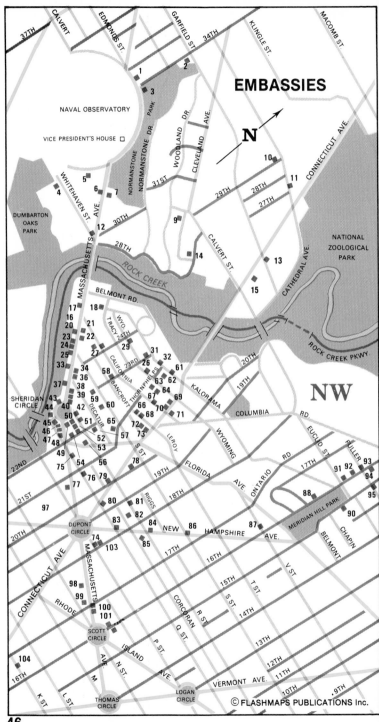

EMBASSIES

N

NW

© FLASHMAPS PUBLICATIONS Inc.

46

EMBASSIES—BY MAP NUMBER

1	Cape Verde	26	Syria	53	Niger	79	Malawi
1	Norway	27	Yugoslavia	54	Cen Africa Rep	80	Lesotho
2	Belgium	29	Afghanistan	54	Bulgaria	81	Sierra Leone
3	Vatican	31	Thailand	56	Mali	82	Singapore
4	Denmark	32	USSR	57	Dominican Rep	83	Argentina
5	New Zealand	33	Malaysia	58	El Salvador	84	Grenada
6	Great Britain	34	Cameroon	59	Burma	84	Rwanda
7	South Africa	36	Austria	60	Laos	85	Nicaragua
9	Panama	37	Oman	62	Ethiopia	86	Zaire
10	Switzerland	37	Upper Volta	63	Sri Lanka	88	Ghana
11	Benin	38	Pakistan	64	Barbados	90	Ecuador
12	Bolivia	39	Haiti	65	Costa Rica	91	Lithuania
12	Brazil	40	Egypt	66	Nepal	92	Poland
14	Lebanon	42	Kenya	67	Algeria	93	Italy
15	China	43	Korea	68	Mauritania	94	Mexico
16	Canada	44	Turkey	69	Senegal	95	Spain
17	Japan	45	Romania	70	Iceland	97	Mozambique
18	Guyana	46	Ireland	71	Malta	98	Chile
18	Portugal	47	Luxembourg	72	Colombia	98	Germany (East)
20	Ivory Coast	48	Suda	73	Guinea	99	Trinidad
21	Venezuela	48	Togo	74	Iraq	100	Peru
22	Zambia	49	Guatemala	75	India	101	Philippines
23	Tunisia	50	Cyprus	76	Morocco	102	Australia
24	Paraguay	51	Greece	77	Indonesia	104	Dominica
25	Madagascar	52	Tanzania	78	Gabon		

EMBASSIES—ALPHABETICAL

Embassy	Address	Map No	Telephone
Afghanistan	2001 24th Street NW	29	234-3770
Algeria	2118 Kalorama	67	328-5300
Argentina	1600 New Hampshire NW	83	387-0705
Australia	1601 Massachusetts NW	102	797-3000
Austria	2343 Massachusetts NW	36	483-4474
Bahamas	600 New Hampshire NW	★	338-3940
Bahrain	3502 International Drive	★	342-0741
Bangladesh	2201 Wisconsin Ave NW	★	342-8372
Barbados	2144 Wyoming NW	64	387-7374
Belgium	3330 Garfield NW	2	333-6900
Benin	2737 Cathedral Ave	11	232-6656
Bolivia	3014 Massachusetts NW	12	483-4410
Botswana	4301 Connecticut NW	★	244-4990
Brazil	3006 Massachusetts NW	12	745-2700
Bulgaria	1621 22nd Street NW	87	387-7969
Burma	2300 S Street NW	59	332-9044
Burundi	2233 Wisconsin Ave NW	★	342-2574
Cameroon	2349 Massachusetts NW	34	265-8790
Canada	2450 Massachusetts NW	16	483-5505
Cape Verde	3415 Massachusetts NW	★	965-6820
Central Africa Republic	1618 22nd Street NW	54	483-7800
Chad	2002 R Street NW	★	462-4009
Chile	1736 Massachusetts NW	98	785-1746
China, People's Rep	2300 Connecticut Ave	15	328-2500
Colombia	2118 Leroy Place NW	72	387-8338
Congo	4891 Colorado Ave NW	★	726-5500
Costa Rica	2112 S Street NW	65	234-2945

★ off map

Embassy	Address	Map No	Telephone
Cyprus	2211 R Street NW	50	462-5772
Czechoslovakia	3900 Linnean NW	★	363-6315
Denmark	3200 Whitehaven NW	4	234-4300
Dominica	1629 K Street NW	104	467-5933
Dominican Republic	1715 22nd Street NW	57	332-6280
Ecuador	2535 15th Street NW	90	234-7200
Egypt	2310 Decatur Place NW	40	232-5400
El Salvador	2308 California NW	58	265-3480
Ethiopia	2134 Kalorama NW	62	234-2281
Fiji	2233 Wisconsin Ave NW	★	337-8320
Finland	3216 New Mexico Ave NW	★	363-2430
France	4101 Reservoir Road NW	★	944-6000
Gabon	2034 20th Street NW	78	797-1000
German Dem Rep (East)	1717 Massachusetts Ave NW	98	232-3134
German Fed Rep (West)	4645 Reservoir Road	★	298-4000
Ghana	2460 16th Street NW	88	462-0761
Great Britain	3100 Massachusetts NW	6	462-1340
Greece	2221 Massachusetts NW	51	667-3168
Grenada	1701 New Hampshire NW	84	265-2561
Guatemala	2220 R Street NW	49	745-4952
Guinea	2112 Leroy Place	73	483-9420
Guyana	2490 Tracy Place	18	265-6900
Haiti	2311 Massachusetts NW	39	332-4090
Honduras	4301 Connecticut NW	★	966-7700
Hungary	3910 Shoemaker St NW	★	362-6730
Iceland	2022 Connecticut NW	70	265-6653
India	2107 Massachusetts NW	75	939-7000
Indonesia	2020 Massachusetts NW	77	293-1745
Iraq	1801 P Street NW	74	483-7500
Ireland	2234 Massachusetts NW	46	462-3939
Israel	3514 International Dr NW	★	364-5500
Italy	1601 Fuller Street NW	93	328-5500
Ivory Coast	2424 Massachusetts NW	20	483-2400
Jamaica	1850 K Street NW	★	452-0660
Japan	2520 Massachusetts NW	17	234-2266
Jordan	3504 International Dr NW	★	966-2664
Kenya	2249 R Street NW	42	387-6101
Korea	2320 Massachusetts NW	43	483-7383
Kuwait	2940 Tilden Street	★	966-0702
Laos	2222 S Street NW	60	332-6416
Latvia	4325 17th Street NW	★	726-8213
Lebanon	2560 28th Street NW	14	939-6300
Lesotho	1601 Connecticut NW	80	462-4190
Liberia	5201 16th Street NW	★	291-1711
Lithuania	2622 16th Street NW	91	234-5860
Luxembourg	2200 Massachusetts NW	47	265-4171
Madagascar	2374 Massachusetts NW	25	265-5525
Malawi	1400 20th Street NW	79	296-5530
Malaysia	2401 Massachusetts NW	33	328-2700
Mali	2130 R Street NW	56	332-2249
Malta	2017 Connecticut NW	71	462-3611
Mauritania	2129 Leroy Place	68	232-5700
Mauritius	4301 Connecticut NW	★	244-1491
Mexico	2829 16th Street NW	94	234-6000

★ off map

EMBASSIES—ALPHABETICAL (Continued)

Embassy	Address	Map No	Telephone
Morocco	1601 21st Street NW	76	462-7979
Mozambique	1990 M Street NW	97	293-7146
Nepal	2131 Leroy Place	66	667-4550
Netherlands	4200 Linnean		244-5300
New Zealand	37 Observation Circle	5	328-4800
Nicaragua	1627 New Hampshire NW	85	387-4371
Niger	2204 R Street NW	53	483-4224
Nigeria	2201 M Street NW		822-1500
Norway	2720 34th Street NW	1	333-6000
Oman	2342 Massachusetts NW	37	387-1980
Pakistan	2315 Massachusetts NW	38	332-8330
Panama	2862 McGill Terrace NW	9	483-1407
Paraguay	2400 Massachusetts NW	24	483-6960
Peru	1700 Massachusetts NW	100	833-9860
Philippines	1617 Massachusetts NW	101	483-1414
Poland	2640 16th Street NW	92	234-3800
Portugal	2310 Tracy Pl NW	18	332-3007
Qatar	600 New Hampshire NW		338-0111
Romania	1607 23rd Street NW	45	338-0111
Rwanda	1714 New Hampshire NW	84	232-2882
San Marino	2033 M Street NW		223-3517
Saudi Arabia	601 New Hampshire NW		342-3800
Senegal	2112 Wyoming NW	69	234-0540
Sierra Leone	1701 19th Street NW	81	939-9261
Singapore	1824 R Street NW	82	667-7555
Somalia	600 New Hampshire NW		342-1575
South Africa	3051 Massachusetts NW	7	232-4400
Spain	2700 15th Street NW	95	265-0190
Sri Lanka	2148 Wyoming NW	63	483-4025
St. Lucia	2100 M Street NW		463-7378
Sudan	2210 Massachusetts NW	48	466-6280
Surinam	2600 Virginia NW	★	338-6980
Swaziland	4301 Connecticut NW	★	362-6683
Sweden	600 New Hampshire NW	★	298-3500
Switzerland	2900 Cathedral	10	745-7900
Syria	2215 Wyoming NW	26	232-6313
Tanzania	2139 R Street NW	52	939-6125
Thailand	2300 Kalorama	31	483-7200
Togo	2208 Massachusetts NW	48	234-4212
Trinidad/Tobago	1708 Massachusetts NW	99	467-6490
Tunisia	2408 Massachusetts NW	23	234-6644
Turkey	1606 23rd Street NW	44	387-3200
Uganda	5909 16th Street NW	★	726-7100
United Arab Emirates	600 New Hampshire NW	★	338-6500
Upper Volta	2340 Massachusetts NW	37	332-5577
Uruguay	1918 F Street NW	★	331-1313
U. S. S. R.	1825 Phelps NW	32	332-1466
Vatican	3339 Massachusetts NW	3	333-7121
Venezuela	2445 Massachusetts NW	21	797-3800
Yemen	600 New Hampshire NW	★	965-4760
Yugoslavia	2410 California NW	27	462-6566
Zaire	1800 New Hampshire NW	86	234-7690
Zambia	2419 Massachusetts NW	22	265-9717
Zimbabwe	2852 McGill Terrace NW	★	332-7100

★ off map

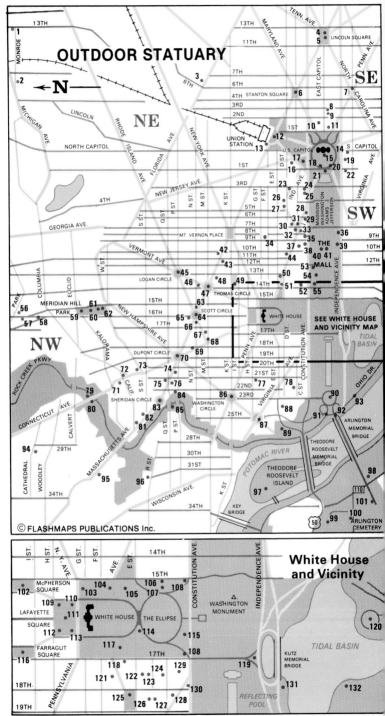

OUTDOOR STATUARY

← **N** →

NE

SE

SW

NW

© FLASHMAPS PUBLICATIONS Inc.

White House and Vicinity

OUTDOOR STATUARY—BY MAP NUMBERS

1 St.Jerome, the Priest	47 Gen George Thomas	93 John Ericsson
2 St. Dominic	48 Christ, Light of World	94 Eurythmy
3 Thomas Gaullaudet	49 Commodore J. Barry	94 Orbit
3 Edward Gaullaudet	50 Gen Count Pulaski	95 Winston Churchill
4 Mary McLeod Bethune	51 Alexander Shepherd	96 Pebble Garden
5 Emancipation Monum.	52 Strauss Fountain	97 Theodore Roosevelt
6 Gen Nathanael Greene	53 Three Red Lines	98 The Hiker
7 Olive Risley Seward	54 Infinity	99 Marine Corps Mem
8 Shakespeare Scenes	55 The Gwenfritz	100 Netherlands Carillon
9 Puck Fountain	56 Cardinal Gibbons	101 Rear Adm Richrd Byrd
10 Law & Justice	57 Marconi Memorial	102 Gen James McPherson
11 The Court of Neptune	58 Francis Asbury	103 Albert Gallatin
11 Ethnological Heads	59 Serenity	104 Alexander Hamilton
12 Columbus Fountain	60 Dante	105 Gen W. T. Sherman
13 Minute Man	61 Joan of Arc	106 Settlers of D.C.
14 Greek Vases	62 James Buchanan	107 Boys Scout Memorial
15 John Marshall	63 Dr Samuel Hahnemann	108 Bullfinch Gatehouses
16 Acacia Griffins	64 Gen Winfield Scott	109 Gen. Kosciuszko
17 Taft Memorial	65 Australian Seal	110 Gen. Lafayette
18 Peace Monument	66 Daniel Webster	111 Andrew Jackson
19 Law & Justice	67 Nuns of Battlefield	112 Baron von Steuben
20 Pres. James Garfield	68 H. W. Longfellow	113 Comte de Rochambeau
21 U.S. Grant Memorial	69 John Witherspoon	114 Butt-Millet Memorial
22 Bartholdi Fountain	70 Dupont Memorial-	115 2nd Div.Memorial
23 Gen. Albert Pike	Daniel Chester French	116 Adm David Farragut
24 Blackstone	71 Habitat	117 1st Div. Memorial
25 Trylon of Freedom	72 Gen Geo. McClellan	118 Canova Lions
26 Abraham Lincoln	73 Cubi XI	119 John Paul Jones
27 Darlington Fountain	74 Balinese Demons	120 Jefferson Memorial
28 Mellon Fountain	75 Braque Bird	121 Architects Memorial
29 Man Controlling Trade	76 Hercules/Buddha/Sphinx	122 Red Cross Memorial
30 Temperance Fountain	77 Ascension	123 Jane A Delano
31 G.A.R. Memorial	78 Expanding Universe	124 D.A.R. Founders
32 Gen.W.S. Hancock	79 Bairstow Lampposts	125 Gen. John Rawlins
33 Past & Future	80 Perry Lions	126 Negro Mother & Child
34 Pegasus& Bellerophon	81 The Prophet	127 Lincoln, Rail Joiner
35 Acroterion Eagles	82 Robert Emmet	128 Gen. Simon Bolivar
36 Burghers of Calais	83 Gen. Philip Sheridan	129 Queen Isabella
37 Robert F. Kennedy	84 Taras Shevchenko	129 South America
38 Capt. Nathan Hale	85 Buffaloes	129 North America
39 A.J. Downing Urn	86 George Washington	129 Aztec Fountain
40 Uncle Beazley	87 Benito Juarez	129 The Prophet Daniel
41 Joseph Henry	88 Dr. Benjamin Rush	129 Jose Cecilio D'Valle
42 Sam Gompers Mem.	89 America-War & Peace	129 Cordell Hull
43 Edmund Burke	90 Lincoln Memorial-	129 Xochipilli,Aztec God
44 Benjamin Franklin	Daniel Chester French	130 Jose Gervasio Artigas
45 Gen. John Logan	91 The Arts of Peace	131 Japanese Lantern
46 Martin Luther	92 The Arts of War	132 Japanese Pagoda

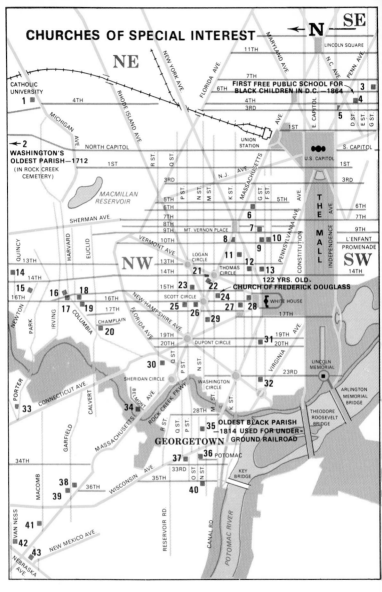

CHURCHES OF SPECIAL INTEREST

NE

SE

← **N**

NW

SW

CATHOLIC UNIVERSITY

← 2 WASHINGTON'S OLDEST PARISH—1712 (IN ROCK CREEK CEMETERY)

FIRST FREE PUBLIC SCHOOL FOR BLACK CHILDREN IN D.C.—1864 →

122 YRS. OLD— CHURCH OF FREDERICK DOUGLASS

WHITE HOUSE

GEORGETOWN

OLDEST BLACK PARISH —1814 USED FOR UNDER-GROUND RAILROAD

MACMILLAN RESERVOIR

UNION STATION

U.S. CAPITOL

THE MALL

L'ENFANT PROMENADE

LINCOLN SQUARE

LINCOLN MEMORIAL

ARLINGTON MEMORIAL BRIDGE

THEODORE ROOSEVELT BRIDGE

KEY BRIDGE

POTOMAC RIVER

CHURCHES PRESIDENTS ATTENDED

3	Thomas Jefferson	28	Franklin Pierce	7	Warren Harding
28	James Madison	12	Abraham Lincoln	9	Calvin Coolidge
28	James Monroe	25	Rutherford B. Hayes	30	Herbert Hoover
28	John Quincy Adams	22	James A. Garfield	26	Harry S. Truman
28	Martin Van Buren	28	Chester A. Arthur	40	John F. Kennedy
28	Wm. Henry Harrison	23	Theodore Roosevelt	22	Lyndon Johnson
28	John Tyler	18	William H Taft	28	Gerald Ford
28	Zachary Taylor	16	Woodrow Wilson	26	Jimmy Carter

CHURCHES OF SPECIAL INTEREST—BY MAP NOS.

1 Shrine Immac	12 NY Av Presby	24 Metro AME	35 Mt. Zion
2 St. Paul's	13 Epiphany	25 Foundry Meth	36 St. John's
3 Christ Church	14 Franciscan	26 First Baptist	37 G'town Luth
4 Ebenezer	15 St. Stephen	27 Third Christ	38 Cath Sophia
5 Capitol Hill	16 Central Presb	28 St. John's	39 Wash Cath
6 St. Mary's	17 Nat'l Baptist	29 St. Matthew's	40 Holy Trinity
7 Calvary Bapt	18 All Souls'	30 Friends Mtg	41 Wash Hebrew
8 Mt. Vernon	19 First Christ	31 Westrn Presby	42 Nat'l Presby
9 First Congr	20 First Christ	32 St. Mary's	43 Metro Mem
10 St. Patrick's	21 Luther Mem	33 Adas Israel	
11 Asbury Meth	22 Nat'l City	34 Islamic	
	23 Grace Evang		

CHURCHES OF SPECIAL INTEREST—ALPHABETICAL

Church	Address	Map No	Telephone
Adas Israel Synagogue	Conn & Porter NW	33	362-4433
All Souls Unitarian	16th & Harvard NW	18	332-5266
Asbury Methodist	11th & K St NW	11	628-0009
Calvary Baptist	8th & H St NW	7	347-8355
Capitol Hill Presbyterian	201 4th St SE	5	547-8676
Cathedral of St. Sophia	36th & Mass NW	38	333-4730
Central Presbyterian (site only)	15th & Irving NW	16	no phone
Christ Church	620 G St SE	3	547-9300
Church of the Epiphany	1317 G St NW	13	347-2635
Ebenezer United Methodist	4th & D St SE	4	544-9539
First Baptist Church	1326 16th St NW	26	387-2206
First Christ Scientist	1770 Euclid NW	20	265-1390
First Congregational	10th & G St NW	9	628-4317
Foundry Methodist	16th & Church NW	25	332-4010
Franciscan Monastery	1400 Quincy NE	14	526-6800
Friends Meeting of Washington	2111 Florida NW	30	483-3310
Georgetown Lutheran	Wisconsin & Volta Pl	37	337-9070
Grace Evangelical & Reform	15th & O St NW	23	387-3131
Holy Trinity Catholic	35th & O St NW	40	337-2840
Islamic Center Mosque	2551 Mass NW	34	332-8343
Luther Place Memorial	Thomas Circle/Vt Ave	21	667-1377
Metropolitan A.M.E.	1518 M St NW	24	331-1426
Metro Memorial Methodist	Nebraska & New Mex	43	363-4900
Mormon Temple, L.D.S.	9900 Stony Brook, Kngstn	off	*589-1435
Mt. Vernon Place Methodist	900 Mass NW	8	347-9620
Mt. Zion United Methodist	1334 29th NW	35	234-0148
National Baptist Memorial	1501 Columbia NW	17	265-1410
National City Christian	Thomas Circle/Mass Av	22	232-0323
National Presbyterian	Nebraska & Van Ness	42	537-0800
New York Ave Presbyterian	1313 New York Ave	12	393-3700
St. John's Episcopal	3240 O St NW	36	338-1796
St. Mary's Catholic	727 5th NW	6	289-7770
St. Mary's Episcopal	728 23rd NW	32	333-3985
St. Matthew's Cathedral	1725 R. I. NW	29	347-3215
St. Patrick's Catholic	619 10th NW	10	347-2713
St. Paul's Rock Creek	Rock Creek Cemetery	2	726-2080
St. Stephen	16th & Newton NW	15	232-0900
Shrine Immaculate Conception	Michigan & 4th NE	1	526-8300
Third Christ Scientist	900 16th NW	27	833-3325
Washington Cathedral	Wis & Mass NW	39	537-6200
Washington Hebrew Congreg.	Macomb & Mass NW	41	362-7100
Western Presbyterian	1906 H St NW	31	842-0068

*Area (301)

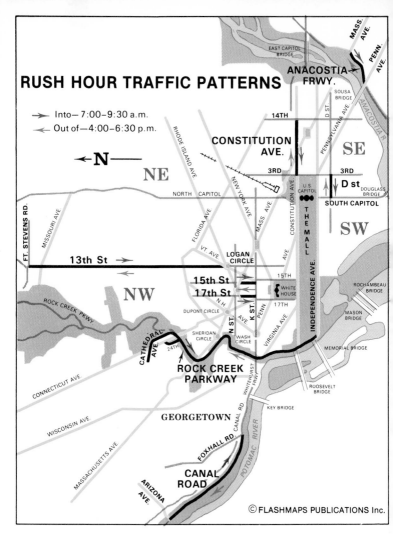

RUSH HOUR TRAFFIC PATTERNS

Into— 7:00–9:30 a.m.
Out of—4:00–6:30 p.m.

← N —

TRAFFIC INFORMATION

Parking Ticket: Fine $15.00 - $100.00
Information for paying fine on back of ticket.
Parking is banned during rush hours 7 to 9:30 AM and 4 to 6:30 PM
on most downtown streets. Fine is $35.
Cars can be towed away during these hours. Fine on the ticket
is then doubled plus towing fee.

Tow-away fee: $25 to $35.

To retrieve car: Call Traffic Division 727-5000

Off street parking: Rates posted at every facility.
Meter rates vary depending on location
Minimum rates from $.75 to $1.00 per hour.

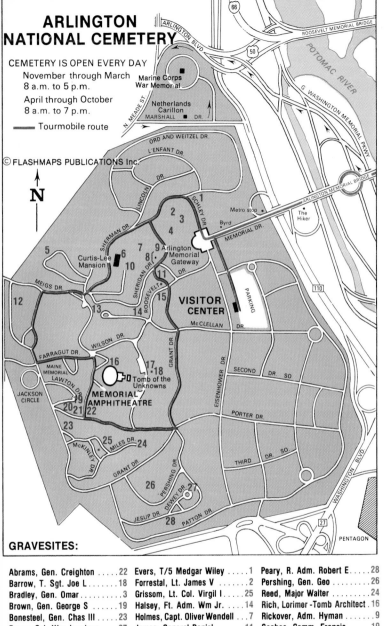

ARLINGTON NATIONAL CEMETERY

CEMETERY IS OPEN EVERY DAY

November through March
8 a.m. to 5 p.m.

April through October
8 a.m. to 7 p.m.

▬▬▬ Tourmobile route

© FLASHMAPS PUBLICATIONS Inc.

N

Marine Corps War Memorial

Netherlands Carillon

ARLINGTON BLVD

ROOSEVELT MEMORIAL BRIDGE

POTOMAC RIVER

G. WASHINGTON MEMORIAL PKWY

N. MEADE ST

MARSHALL DR.

ORD AND WEITZEL DR.

L'ENFANT DR.

LINCOLN DR.

SCHLEY DR.

SHERMAN DR.

Curtis-Lee Mansion

SHERIDAN DR.

ROOSEVELT DR.

MEIGS DR.

WILSON DR.

FARRAGUT DR.

MAINE MEMORIAL

LAWTON DR.

JACKSON CIRCLE

MEMORIAL AMPHITHEATRE

Tomb of the Unknowns

McKINLEY DR.

MILES DR.

GRANT DR.

PERSHING DR.

DEWEY DR.

JESUP DR.

PATTON DR.

Arlington Memorial Gateway

Metro stop

Byrd

The Hiker

MEMORIAL DR.

ARLINGTON MEMORIAL BRIDGE

VISITOR CENTER

PARKING

McCLELLAN DR.

GRANT DR.

EISENHOWER DR.

SECOND DR. SO.

PORTER DR.

THIRD DR. SO.

WASHINGTON BLVD

PENTAGON

GRAVESITES:

55

AVENUES-CIRCLES-PARKS-SQUARES

Constitution Ave	NW	B & 12th
Delaware Ave	NE	D & 1st
Dupont Circle	NW	P & 19th
Farragut Square	NW	H & 17th
Florida Avenue	NW	V & 10th
Folger Park	SE	D & 3rd
Franklin Square	NW	H & 13th
Garfield Park	SE	F & 2nd
Independence Ave	SW	B & 10th
Indiana Ave	NW	D & 6th
Judiciary Square	NW	E & 4th
Kalorama Circle	NW	V & 25th
Lafayette Square	NW	H & 26th
L'Enfant Plaza	SW	D & 9th
Logan Circle	NW	P & 13th
Louisiana Ave	NE	E & N Cap
Maryland Ave	SW	A & 1st
Massachussetts Ave	NW	U & 27th
McPherson Square	NW	H & 15th
Meridian Hill Park	NW	W & 15th
Mt. Vernon Square	NW	Eye & 8th
New Hampshire	NW	T & 16th
New Jersey Ave	NW	R & 4th
Pennsylvania Ave	NW	D & 10th
Pershing Square	NW	D & 14th
Rawlins Park	NW	E & 19th
Rhode Island Ave	NW	R & 7th
Scott Circle	NW	N & 16th
Sheridan Circle	NW	R & 24th
Thomas Circle	NW	M & 14th
Union Station Pl	NE	E & N Cap
Vermont Ave	NW	V & 10th
Virginia Ave	NW	D & 22nd
Washington Circle	NW	K & 23rd
W Potomac Park	NW	B & 20th

© FLASHMAPS PUBLICATIONS Inc.

57

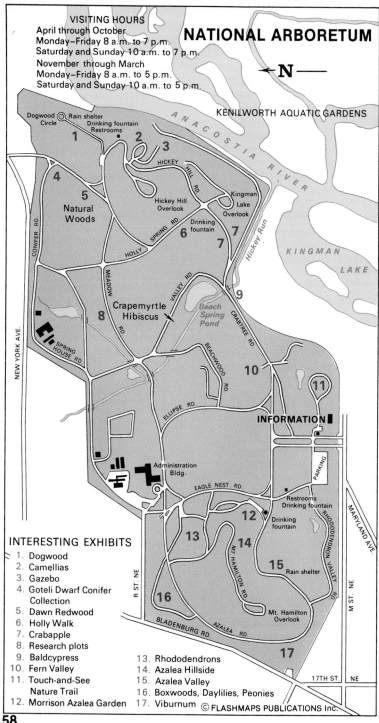

VISITING HOURS
April through October
Monday–Friday 8 a.m. to 7 p.m.
Saturday and Sunday 10 a.m. to 7 p.m.
November through March
Monday–Friday 8 a.m. to 5 p.m.
Saturday and Sunday 10 a.m. to 5 p.m.

KENILWORTH AQUATIC GARDENS

ANACOSTIA RIVER

Dogwood Circle
Rain shelter
Drinking fountain
Restrooms

1

2

3

HICKEY
HILL RD.

4

5

Natural Woods

Hickey Hill Overlook

Kingman Lake Overlook

SPRING RD.

HOLLY

6

Drinking fountain

7

7

Hickey Run

KINGMAN LAKE

CONIFER RD.

MEADOW RD.

VALLEY RD.

Crapemyrtle Hibiscus

8

SPRING HOUSE RD.

NEW YORK AVE.

Beach Spring Pond

9

CRABTREE RD.

BEACHWOOD RD.

10

11

ELLIPSE RD.

INFORMATION

PARKING

Administration Bldg.

EAGLE NEST RD.

Restrooms
Drinking fountain

RHODODENDRON VALLEY RD.

MARYLAND AVE.

12

Drinking fountain

R ST. NE

13

14

15

Rain shelter

MT. HAMILTON RD.

16

Mt. Hamilton Overlook

M ST. NE

BLADENBURG RD.

AZALEA RD.

17

17TH ST. NE

INTERESTING EXHIBITS

1. Dogwood
2. Camellias
3. Gazebo
4. Goteli Dwarf Conifer Collection
5. Dawn Redwood
6. Holly Walk
7. Crabapple
8. Research plots
9. Baldcypress
10. Fern Valley
11. Touch-and-See Nature Trail
12. Morrison Azalea Garden
13. Rhododendrons
14. Azalea Hillside
15. Azalea Valley
16. Boxwoods, Daylilies, Peonies
17. Viburnum

© FLASHMAPS PUBLICATIONS Inc.

58

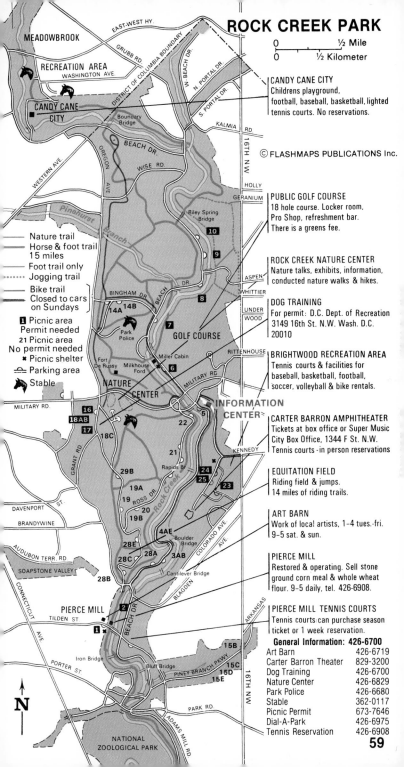

ROCK CREEK PARK

0 ½ Mile
0 ½ Kilometer

© FLASHMAPS PUBLICATIONS Inc.

CANDY CANE CITY
Childrens playground,
football, baseball, basketball, lighted
tennis courts. No reservations.

PUBLIC GOLF COURSE
18 hole course. Locker room,
Pro Shop, refreshment bar.
There is a greens fee.

ROCK CREEK NATURE CENTER
Nature talks, exhibits, information,
conducted nature walks & hikes.

DOG TRAINING
For permit: D.C. Dept. of Recreation
3149 16th St. N.W. Wash. D.C.
20010

BRIGHTWOOD RECREATION AREA
Tennis courts & facilities for
baseball, basketball, football,
soccer, volleyball & bike rentals.

CARTER BARRON AMPHITHEATER
Tickets at box office or Super Music
City Box Office, 1344 F St. N.W.
Tennis courts -in person reservations

EQUITATION FIELD
Riding field & jumps.
14 miles of riding trails.

ART BARN
Work of local artists, 1-4 tues.-fri.
9-5 sat. & sun.

PIERCE MILL
Restored & operating. Sell stone
ground corn meal & whole wheat
flour. 9-5 daily, tel. 426-6908.

PIERCE MILL TENNIS COURTS
Tennis courts can purchase season
ticket or 1 week reservation.

General Information: 426-6700
Art Barn	426-6719
Carter Barron Theater	829-3200
Dog Training	426-6700
Nature Center	426-6829
Park Police	426-6680
Stable	362-0117
Picnic Permit	673-7646
Dial-A-Park	426-6975
Tennis Reservation	426-6908

Legend:
Nature trail
Horse & foot trail 15 miles
Foot trail only
Jogging trail
Bike trail
Closed to cars on Sundays
1 Picnic area Permit needed
21 Picnic area No permit needed
× Picnic shelter
⚓ Parking area
🐎 Stable

MEADOWBROOK
RECREATION AREA
Washington Ave.
CANDY CANE CITY
NATURE CENTER
GOLF COURSE
INFORMATION CENTER
PIERCE MILL
NATIONAL ZOOLOGICAL PARK

N

NATIONAL ZOOLOGICAL PARK

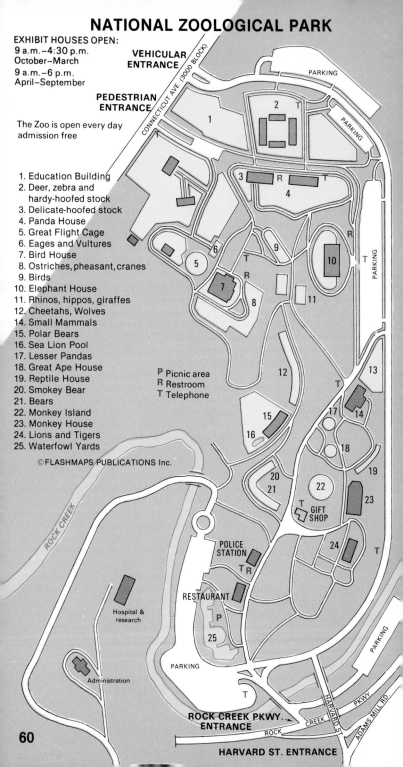

EXHIBIT HOUSES OPEN:
9 a.m.–4:30 p.m.
October–March

9 a.m.–6 p.m.
April–September

The Zoo is open every day
admission free

1. Education Building
2. Deer, zebra and hardy-hoofed stock
3. Delicate-hoofed stock
4. Panda House
5. Great Flight Cage
6. Eages and Vultures
7. Bird House
8. Ostriches, pheasant, cranes
9. Birds
10. Elephant House
11. Rhinos, hippos, giraffes
12. Cheetahs, Wolves
14. Small Mammals
15. Polar Bears
16. Sea Lion Pool
17. Lesser Pandas
18. Great Ape House
19. Reptile House
20. Smokey Bear
21. Bears
22. Monkey Island
23. Monkey House
24. Lions and Tigers
25. Waterfowl Yards

P Picnic area
R Restroom
T Telephone

©FLASHMAPS PUBLICATIONS Inc.

VEHICULAR ENTRANCE

PEDESTRIAN ENTRANCE

CONNECTICUT AVE (3000 BLOCK)

PARKING

ROCK CREEK

Hospital & research

Administration

POLICE STATION

RESTAURANT

GIFT SHOP

ROCK CREEK PKWY. ENTRANCE

HARVARD ST. ENTRANCE

HARVARD ST.

ADAMS MILL RD.

LANDMARK DAY TRIPS
Harpers Ferry ● Mount Vernon ● Annapolis ● Wolf Trap Farm

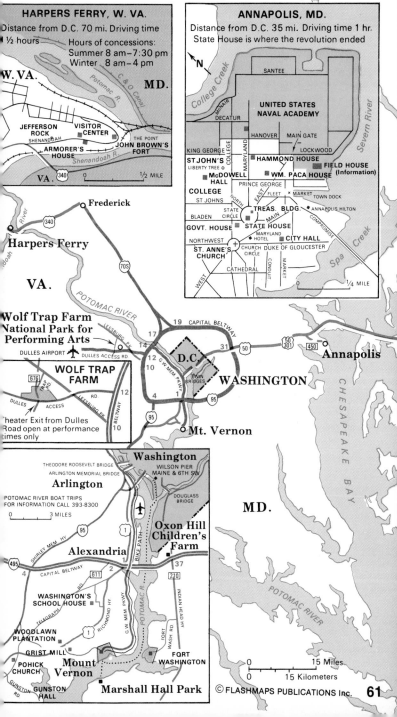

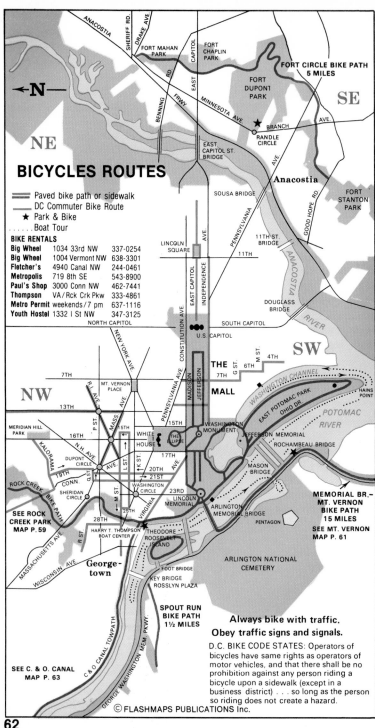

BICYCLES ROUTES

≡≡ Paved bike path or sidewalk
— DC Commuter Bike Route
★ Park & Bike
······ Boat Tour

BIKE RENTALS

Big Wheel	1034 33rd NW	337-0254
Big Wheel	1004 Vermont NW	638-3301
Fletcher's	4940 Canal NW	244-0461
Metropolis	719 8th SE	543-8900
Paul's Shop	3000 Conn NW	462-7441
Thompson	VA/Rck Crk Pkw	333-4861
Metro Permit	weekends/7 pm	637-1116
Youth Hostel	1332 I St NW	347-3125

← **N** —

NE

SE

SW

NW

ANACOSTIA RD.
SHERIFF RD.
DRAKE AVE.
FORT MAHAN PARK
EAST CAPITOL
FORT CHAPLIN PARK
FORT DUPONT PARK
FORT CIRCLE BIKE PATH 5 MILES
BENNING FRWY.
MINNESOTA AVE.
BRANCH
RANDLE CIRCLE
AVE.
Anacostia
FORT STANTON PARK
EAST CAPITOL ST. BRIDGE
GOOD HOPE RD.
SOUSA BRIDGE
PENNSYLVANIA AVE.
11TH ST. BRIDGE
ANACOSTIA RIVER
LINCOLN SQUARE
AVE.
EAST CAPITOL
INDEPENDENCE
11TH
DOUGLASS BRIDGE
SOUTH CAPITOL
U.S. CAPITOL
NORTH CAPITOL
NEW YORK AVE.
CONSTITUTION AVE.
MADISON
JEFFERSON
THE MALL
G ST.
M ST.
4TH
6TH
7TH
WASHINGTON CHANNEL
EAST POTOMAC PARK
OHIO DR.
HAINS POINT
POTOMAC RIVER
7TH
MT. VERNON PLACE
13TH
R.I. AVE.
MASS.
PENNSYLVANIA AVE.
WASHINGTON MONUMENT
JEFFERSON MEMORIAL
ROCHAMBEAU BRIDGE
MERIDIAN HILL PARK
16TH
15TH
WHITE HOUSE
THE ELLIPSE
17TH AVE.
MASON BRIDGE
KALORAMA
N.H. AVE.
DUPONT CIRCLE
L ST.
K ST.
20TH
21ST
MEMORIAL BR.– MT. VERNON BIKE PATH 15 MILES
19TH
CONN.
ROCK CREEK BIKE PATH
SHERIDAN CIRCLE
Q ST.
M ST.
WASHINGTON CIRCLE
23RD
LINCOLN MEMORIAL
ARLINGTON MEMORIAL BRIDGE
PENTAGON
SEE MT. VERNON MAP P. 61
SEE ROCK CREEK PARK MAP P. 59
MASSACHUSETTS AVE.
28TH
R ST.
HARRY T. THOMPSON BOAT CENTER
VIRGINIA
25TH
THEODORE ROOSEVELT ISLAND
ARLINGTON NATIONAL CEMETERY
WISCONSIN AVE.
George-town
FOOT BRIDGE
KEY BRIDGE
ROSSLYN PLAZA
SPOUT RUN BIKE PATH 1½ MILES
C. & O. CANAL TOWPATH
GEORGE WASHINGTON MEM. PKWY.
SEE C. & O. CANAL MAP P. 63

Always bike with traffic.
Obey traffic signs and signals.

D.C. BIKE CODE STATES: Operators of bicycles have same rights as operators of motor vehicles, and that there shall be no prohibition against any person riding a bicycle upon a sidewalk (except in a business district) . . . so long as the person so riding does not create a hazard.

© FLASHMAPS PUBLICATIONS Inc.

62

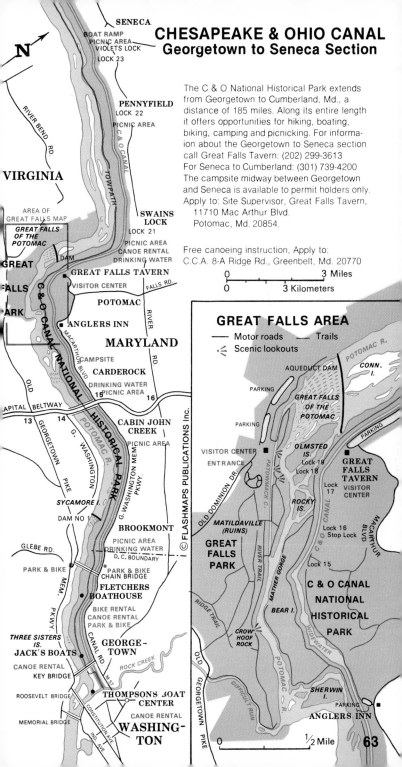

CHESAPEAKE & OHIO CANAL
Georgetown to Seneca Section

The C & O National Historical Park extends from Georgetown to Cumberland, Md., a distance of 185 miles. Along its entire length it offers opportunities for hiking, boating, biking, camping and picnicking. For information about the Georgetown to Seneca section call Great Falls Tavern: (202) 299-3613 For Seneca to Cumberland: (301) 739-4200 The campsite midway between Georgetown and Seneca is available to permit holders only. Apply to: Site Supervisor, Great Falls Tavern,
    11710 Mac Arthur Blvd.
    Potomac, Md. 20854.

Free canoeing instruction, Apply to:
C.C.A. 8-A Ridge Rd., Greenbelt, Md. 20770

0   3 Miles
0   3 Kilometers

GREAT FALLS AREA

— Motor roads   — Trails
Scenic lookouts

0   1/2 Mile

63

NATIONAL TREASURES—BY CATEGORY

ART—PAINTINGS

ART — SCULPTURE

NATIONAL TREASURES—BY CATEGORY

ART—SCULPTURE Continued

		Page
French, Daniel Chester — "Lincoln"	**Lincoln Memorial**	18
Maillol, Aristide — "Action in Chains"	**Hirshhorn Museum**	18
Matisse — "Backs"	**Hirshhorn Museum**	18
Moore, Henry — "King and Queen"	**Hirshhorn Museum**	18
Moore, Henry — "Knife Edge Mirror Two Piece"	**National Gallery**	18
Noguchi, Isamu — "Great Rock of Inner Seeking"	**National Gallery**	18
Rodin — "Burghers of Calais" and "Tribute to Balzac"	**Hirshhorn Mus**	18
Saint-Gaudens, Augustus — "Grief"	**St Paul's Church**	52
Verrocchio — "Lorenzo de Medici"	**National Gallery**	18

ART—RARE COLLECTIONS

African Art — Sculpture and textiles	**African Art Museum**	76
American Antiques (Diplomatic reception rooms)	**State Department**	16
Byzantine and Early Christian Art	**Dumbarton Oaks**	76
Egyptian Gold Work	**Freer Gallery**	18
Japanese Screens — 17th Century	**Freer Gallery**	18
Judaic ceremonial objects	**B'nai Brith Library**	70
Near Eastern paintings	**Freer Gallery**	18
Oriental Rugs	**Textile Museum**	76
Peacock Room/Paintings — James McNeil Whistler	**Freer Gallery**	18
Pre-Columbian Art	**Dumbarton Oaks**	76
Religious mosaics	**Shrine Immaculate Con**	52
Stradivarius violins & antique musical instruments	**Freer Gallery**	18

HISTORICAL

Bible of Mainz — (1453)	**Library of Congress**	16
Bill of Rights	**Archives**	16
Congress Bells — replica of Westminster 1596 bells	**Old Post Office**	16
Constitution of the United States of America	**Archives**	16
Declaration of Independence — First draft	**Library of Congress**	16
Early maps	**Library of Congress**	16
Elizabethan theater	**Folger Library**	18
First Ladies' ball gowns	**Museum American History**	18
Gutenberg Bible — (1455)	**Library of Congress**	16
Lincoln's Gettysburg Address — 1st & 2nd drafts	**Library of Congress**	16
Matthew Brady photographs	**Library of Congress**	16
Presidents' papers: Washington, Jefferson, Lincoln, Wilson	**Lib Congrss**	16
Revolutionary War memorabilia	**Anderson House**	76
Shakespeare first folios	**Folger Library**	18
Star Spangled Banner (original)	**Mus American History**	18
United Nations Charter	**Archives**	16

SCIENTIFIC

Antique guns	**National Rifle Assoc**	76
Aquarium — 2,000 species exotic fish	**National Aquarium**	76
Atomic clock	**Naval Observatory**	76
Benjamin Franklin's printing press	**Mus of American History**	18
Edison's electric lamp	**Mus of American History**	18
Earlybird satellite	**Air & Space Museum**	18
Foucault pendulum	**Mus of American History**	18
Gems — Hope Diamond, Star of Asia Sapphire	**Mus Natural History**	18
Kitty Hawk Flyer — Wright Brothers	**Air & Space Museum**	18
Lunar Rock	**Air & Space Museum**	18
Space Craft — Friendship 7, Apollo II, Discoverer 13	**Air & Space**	18
Spirit of St Louis	**Air & Space Museum**	18

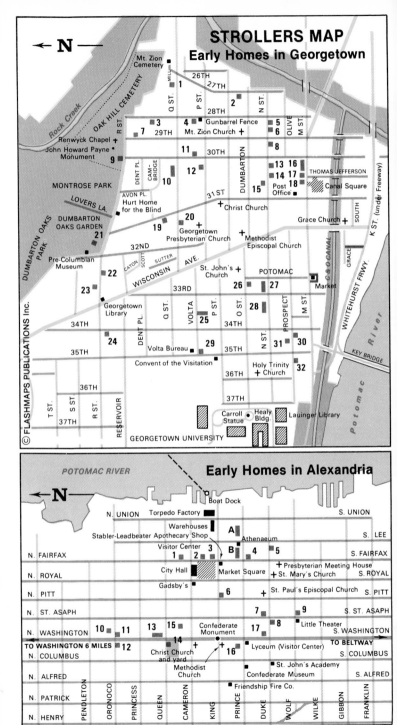

STROLLERS MAP
Early Homes in Georgetown

← N →

Mt. Zion Cemetery
Rock Creek
OAK HILL CEMETERY
MILL
Q ST.
P ST.
N ST.
26TH
27TH
1
2
28TH
3
4 Gunbarrel Fence
5
6
7 Mt. Zion Church ✝
OLIVE
M ST.
8
29TH
Renwyck Chapel ✝
John Howard Payne Monument
9
11
30TH
12
13 16
14 17
DENT PL.
CAM-BRIDGE
10
DUMBARTON
15 Post Office
18
THOMAS JEFFERSON
Canal Square
MONTROSE PARK
LOVERS LA.
AVON PL.
Hurt Home for the Blind
31 ST
✝ Christ Church
SOUTH
Grace Church ✝
19 20 Georgetown Presbyterian Church
✝ Methodist Episcopal Church
DUMBARTON OAKS GARDEN
21
DUMBARTON OAKS PARK
32ND
CATON
SCOTT
SUTTER
WISCONSIN AVE.
St. John's Church
POTOMAC
GRACE
K ST. (under Freeway)
C & O CANAL
WHITEHURST FRWY.
Pre-Columbian Museum
22
26
27 Market
23
33RD
28
Georgetown Library
Q ST.
VOLTA
P ST.
O ST.
25
PROSPECT
M ST.
River
Potomac
34TH
DENT PL.
34TH
24
Volta Bureau
29
N ST.
31
30
KEY BRIDGE
35TH
35TH
Convent of the Visitation
36TH
Holy Trinity ✝ Church
32
© FLASHMAPS PUBLICATIONS Inc.
T ST.
S ST.
R ST.
37TH
RESERVOIR
36TH
37TH
Carroll Statue
Healy Bldg.
Lauinger Library
GEORGETOWN UNIVERSITY

POTOMAC RIVER
Early Homes in Alexandria
← N →
Boat Dock
N. UNION Torpedo Factory S. UNION
Warehouses
Stabler-Leadbeater Apothecary Shop
A Athenaeum
S. LEE
N. FAIRFAX Visitor Center 1 2 3 B 4 5 S. FAIRFAX
City Hall
N. ROYAL Market Square ✝ Presbyterian Meeting House ✝ St. Mary's Church S. ROYAL
Gadsby's
N. PITT 6 ✝ St. Paul's Episcopal Church S. PITT
N. ST. ASAPH 7 9 S. ST. ASAPH
Confederate Monument
N. WASHINGTON 10 11 13 15 17 8 Little Theater S. WASHINGTON
TO WASHINGTON 6 MILES 12 14 16 Lyceum (Visitor Center) TO BELTWAY
N. COLUMBUS Christ Church and yard ✝ ✝ St. John's Academy S. COLUMBUS
N. ALFRED Methodist Church Confederate Museum S. ALFRED
Friendship Fire Co.
N. PATRICK
PENDLETON
ORONOCO
PRINCESS
QUEEN
CAMERON
KING
PRINCE
DUKE
WOLF
WILKE
GIBBON
FRANKLIN
N. HENRY

66

GEORGETOWN HOUSES—BY MAP NUMBER

Map No.	House	Address	Architect	Date
1	Dumbarton House	2715 Q	Benjamin Latrobe	1805
2	Trentman House	1350 27th	H. N. Jacobsen	1968
3	Evermay	1628 28th	Nicholas King	1801
4	Miller House	1524 28th	Benjamin Miller	1840
5	Gannt-Williams House	2806 N	Unknown	1817
6	Decatur House	2812 N	J. S. Williams	1813
7	Mackall Square	1633 29th	Benjamin Mackall	1820
8	Foxall House	2908 N	Henry Foxall	c1820
9	Oak Hill Cem Gatehouse	30th & R	de la Roche	1850
10	Cooke's Row	3007-29 Q	Starkweather-Plowman	1868
11	Francis Dodge House	1517 30th	Downing & Vaux	1852
12	Linthicum House	3019 P	Edward Linthicum	1829
13	Laird-Dunlop House	3014 N	William Lovering	1799
14	Riggs-Riley House	3038 N	Romulus Riggs	1816
15	Wheatley House	3041-43 N	Francis Wheatley	1859
16	Thomas Sim Lee Corner	3001-9 M	Unknown	1794
17	Loughboro-Patterson	3039-41 N	Unknown	1801
18	Old Stone House	3051 M	Christopher Layhman	1766
19	Tudor Place	1644 31st	Dr. Wm. Thornton	1815
20	Bowie-Sevier House	3124 Q	Washington Bowie	1805
21	Dumbarton Oaks	3101 R	William H. Dorsey	1801
22	Scott-Grant House	3238 R	A.V. Scott	1858
23	Dougall House	3259 R	Adams & Haskins	1854
24	Mackall-Worthington	1686 34th	Leonard Mackall	1820
25	Pomander Walk	Volta Place	Unknown	1885
26	Bodisco House	3222 O	Clement Smith	1815
27	Smith Row	3255-63 N	W. & C. Smith	1815
28	Cox's Row	3327-39 N	John Cox	1817
29	Alexander Melville Bell	1525 35th	Unknown	c1850
30	Halcyon House	3400 Prospect	Benjamin Stoddert	1787
31	"Quality Hill"	3425 Prospect	J.T.Mason	1798
32	Prospect House	3508 Prospect	J. M. Lingan	1788

EARLY ALEXANDRIA HOUSES—BY MAP NUMBER

Map No.	House	Address	Date
1	Thompson-Marshburn House	211 N Fairfax	1799
2	Carlyle House	121 N Fairfax	1752
3	Ramsay House	King & Fairfax	1749
4	Dr. William Brown House	212 S. Fairfax	1775
5	Dr. James Craik House	210 Duke	1789
6	Marshall House	King & Pitt	c1850
7	Dulaney House	601 Duke	1785
8	Lawrason-Lafayette House	Duke & S. St. Asaph	1820
9	Vowell-Smith House	Wolfe & S. St. Asaph	1840
10	Robert E. Lee House	607 Oronoco	1795
11	Fendall-John L. Lewis House	614 Oronoco	c1800
12	Edmund Jennings Lee House	Oronoco & N. Wash.	1800
13	Brockett's Row	301-7 N. Wash.	1840
14	Lloyd House	Queen & N. Wash.	c1793
15	Yeaton-Fairfax House	607 Cameron	1799
16	William Fowle House	711 Prince	c1800
17	Lloyd's Row	220-28 S. Wash.	1811

A. B. Captain's Row & Prince Street Row Houses, 18th Century

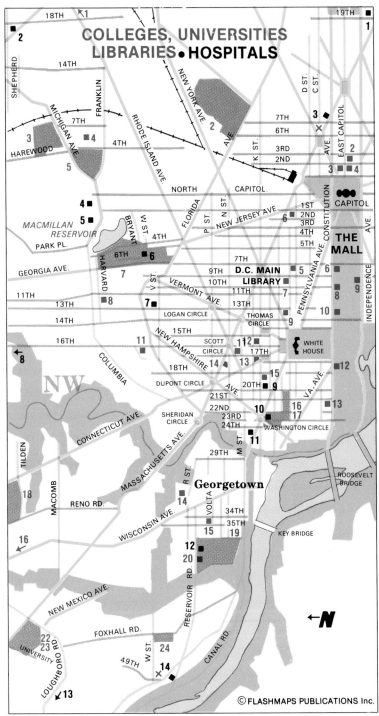

COLLEGES, UNIVERSITIES
LIBRARIES • HOSPITALS

© FLASHMAPS PUBLICATIONS Inc.

HOSPITALS • COLLEGES • LIBRARIES — BY MAP NO.

HOSPITALS • COLLEGES • LIBRARIES

HOSPITAL	Address	Map No.	Telephone
Capitol Hill	708 Mass NE	3	269-8000
Columbia Hospital for Women	2425 L St NW	11	293-6500
Children's	111 Michigan Ave NW	7	745-5000
D. C. General	Mass Ave & 19th St SE	1	675-5000
Geo Washington Univ Med Ctr	901 23rd St NW	10	676-6000
Georgetown University	3800 Reservoir Rd	12	625-0100
Greater Southeast Community	1310 Southern Ave SE	★	574-6000
Hadley	4601 Martin Luther King SW	★	574-5700
Howard University	2041 Georgia Ave NW	6	745-6100
Providence	1150 Varnum NE	★	269-7000
Psychiatric Institute	4460 Mac Arthur Blvd NW	14	944-3400
Sibley	5255 Loughboro Rd NW	13	537-4000
Sick Children's Hospital	1731 Bunker Hill Rd	2	832-4400
St. Elizabeth's	Congress Heights	★	562-4000
Veteran's Administration	50 Irving NW	4	745-8000
Walter Reed	6825 16th St NW	8	545-6700
Washington Hospital Center	110 Irving NW	5	541-0500

COLLEGE/UNIVERSITY			
American University	Mass & Nebraska NW	22	686-2000
Antioch School of Law	1624 Crescent Pl NW	11	265-9500
Benjamin Franklin Univ	1100 Sixteenth NW	12	737-2262
Berlitz School of Languages	1050 17th St NW	13	331-1160
Catholic Univ of America	620 Michigan NE	3	635-5000
D. C. Teachers College	1100 Harvard NW	8	282-7300
Federal City Univ DC	1st & D St NW	9	282-7300
Gallaudet College	Florida & 7th St NE	2	651-5000
George Washington Univ	2121 1st St NW	17	676-6000
GWU Schl of Engineering	801 22nd Street NW	17	676-6158
GWU Schl of Medicine	2300 Eye St NW	16	676-6000
Georgetown University	O & 37th St NW	19	625-0100
Georgetown International	1800 K St NW	15	887-0200
Georgetown Law Center	600 New Jersey NW	6	624-8000

★ off map

HOSPITALS • COLLEGES • LIBRARIES — Continued

COLLEGE/UNIVERSITY

	Address	Map No.	Telephone
Georgetown Schl of Med	3900 Reservoir Road NW	20	625-0100
Georgetown Schl of Nursing	3700 Reservoir Road NW	20	625-0100
Howard University	2400 6th St NW	7	636-6100
Johns Hopkins Internat'l Univ	1740 Mass NW	14	785-6200
Mount Vernon College	2100 Foxhall Rd NW	24	331-0400
National War College	Fort McNair	off	545-6700
St. Paul's College	3015 4th St NE	4	832-6262
Trinity College	Michigan & Franklin St NE	5	939-5000
University of D.C.	4200 Conn NW	18	282-7300
Wesley Theological Institute	4400 Mass NW	23	885-8600

LIBRARY

	Address	Map No.	Telephone
Arts and Industries	The Mall	9	357-1300
Board of Ed Sumner Research	17th & M Street NW	11	727-3419
B'nai B'rith "Four Freedoms"	1640 Rhode Island NW	11	857-6600
Collection of Fine Arts	G St & 8th NW	5	357-1300
Dumbarton Oaks Garden	1703 32nd St NW	14	342-3240
Folger Shakespeare	201 East Capitol	2	544-4600
History and Technology	The Mall	10	357-1300
Library of Congress	10 1st St SE	4	287-5000
Martin Luther King Memorial	901 G St NW	7	727-1111
National Academy Sciences	2101 Constitution NW	13	393-8100
National Agricultural	Beltsville, Maryland	1	*344-3755
National Archives	Penn Ave & 8th St NW	6	655-4000
National Medical	600 Rockville Pk, Rockville	16	496-6095
Natural History	The Mall	8	357-1300
OAS Columbus Memorial	Constitution & 17th St NW	12	331-1010
Supreme Court	1st St & East Capitol NE	3	479-3175
Volta Bureau	1537 35th St NW	15	337-5220

★ Area (301)

MAJOR STORES IN SHOPPING CENTERS (Map Page 71)

CHEVY CHASE / MAZZA—WOODWARD & LOTHROP, LORD & TAYLOR, SAKS FIFTH AVE, GUCCI NEIMAN MARCUS, ANN TAYLOR, F A O SCHWARZ, SAINT-LAURENT, CHAS SCHWARTZ

DOWNTOWN DC—GARFINCKEL'S, LORD & TAYLOR, W. J. SLOANE, ARTHUR ADLER, HECHT'S, RALEIGHS, CASUAL CORNER, ARTHUR ASHE TENNIS, S. KLEIN, MORTON'S, BRENTANO'S, THE PAVILION - 30 SPECIALTY SHOPS, THE SHOPS AT NATIONAL PLACE - 85 SHOPS

GEORGETOWN—THE PHOENIX, GEORGETOWN LEATHER DESIGN, THE FRENCH SHOP, BRITCHES, PAPPAGALLO, ANN TAYLOR, DOROTHY STEAD, SAINT-AUBIN, GEORGETOWN UNIVERSITY SHOP GEORGETOWN PARK - 100 RETAIL SHOPS

LANDMARK—HECHT'S, SEARS, RALEIGHS, CASUAL CORNER, GEORGETOWN LEATHER DESIGN

LANDOVER—GARFINCKEL'S, WOODWARD & LOTHROP, SEARS, HECHT'S, GORDONS, RALEIGHS CASUAL CORNER, SEVEN & NINE, BAILEY BANKS & BIDDLE, B. DALTON, KAY JEWELERS

MONTGOMERY—GARFINCKEL'S, WOODWARD & LOTHROP, SCANDINAVIAN COLLECTION, SEARS, HECHT'S, BAILEY BANKS & BIDDLE, CAMALIER & BUCKLEY, BRITCHES, RALEIGHS

PRINCE GEORGE—WOODWARD & LOTHROP, HECHT'S, RALEIGHS, WILSONS, MURPHYS, UPS N' DOWNS, LANE BRYANT, IRVIN'S SPORT, THE LIMITED, WOOLWORTH'S

SEVEN CORNERS—GARFINCKEL'S, WOODWARD & LOTHROP, W. & J. SLOANE, LERNERS

SPRINGFIELD—GARFINCKEL'S, RALEIGHS, MONTGOMERY WARD, J.C. PENNEY, BRITCHES, YOUNG FAIR, PHILIPS, CASUAL CORNER, GEORGETOWN LEATHER, B.DALTON, THE LIMITED

TYSON'S CORNER—GARFINCKEL'S, WOODWARD & LOTHROP, BLOOMINGDALE'S, HECHT'S ANN TAYLOR, GEORGETOWN LEATHER, CRABTREE & EVELYN, RALEIGHS, B, BANKS & BIDDLE

WATERGATE—AFAF BOUTIQUE, ST. LAURENT, VALENTINO, COLETTE, SAKS-JANDEL, GUCCI

WHITE FLINT—BLOOMINGDALE'S, LORD & TAYLOR, I. MAGNIN, ALFRED DUNHILL, SAINT LAURENT RALEIGHS , CRABTREE & EVELYN, BLACK STAR & FROST, ANN TAYLOR, GEORGETOWN LEATHER

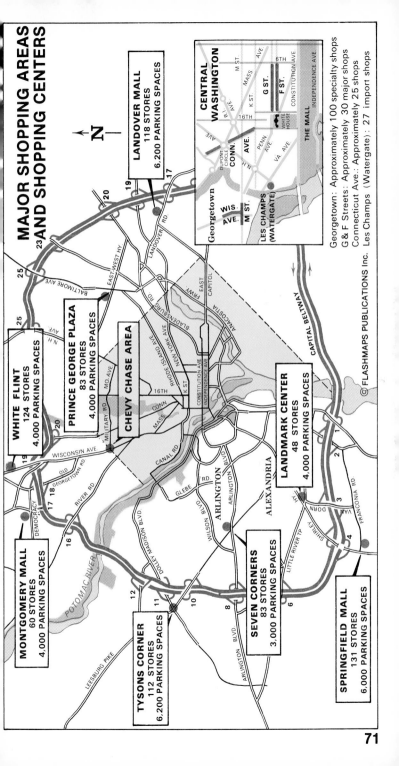

MAJOR SHOPPING AREAS AND SHOPPING CENTERS

← N

LANDOVER MALL
118 STORES
6,200 PARKING SPACES

CENTRAL WASHINGTON

Georgetown
WIS. AVE.
M ST.
Dupont Circle
CONN. AVE.
R AVE.
N AVE.
K ST.
M ST.
MASS. AVE.
16TH
White House
PENN. AVE.
G ST.
F ST.
6TH
CONSTITUTION AVE.
VA. AVE.
INDEPENDENCE AVE.
THE MALL
LES CHAMPS (WATERGATE)

Georgetown: Approximately 100 specialty shops
G & F Streets: Approximately 30 major shops
Connecticut Ave.: Approximately 25 shops
Les Champs (Watergate) : 27 import shops

WHITE FLINT
124 STORES
4,000 PARKING SPACES

PRINCE GEORGE PLAZA
83 STORES
4,000 PARKING SPACES

CHEVY CHASE AREA

MONTGOMERY MALL
60 STORES
4,000 PARKING SPACES

TYSONS CORNER
112 STORES
6,200 PARKING SPACES

SEVEN CORNERS
83 STORES
3,000 PARKING SPACES

LANDMARK CENTER
48 STORES
4,000 PARKING SPACES

SPRINGFIELD MALL
131 STORES
6,000 PARKING SPACES

© FLASHMAPS PUBLICATIONS Inc.

EAST-WEST HWY.
BALTIMORE AVE.
LANDOVER RD.
CAPITAL BELTWAY
EAST CAPITOL FRWY.
BLADENSBURG RD.
NEW YORK AVE.
RHODE ISLAND AVE.
MO. AVE.
CONN.
MASS.
16TH
K ST.
CONSTITUTION AVE.
INDEPENDENCE AVE.
ANACOSTIA
MILITARY RD.
WISCONSIN AVE.
OLD GEORGETOWN RD.
RIVER RD.
DEMOCRACY
CANAL RD.
POTOMAC RIVER
LEESBURG PIKE
DOLLEY MADISON BLVD.
ARLINGTON BLVD.
GLEBE RD.
WILSON BLVD.
ARLINGTON
ARLINGTON BLVD.
LITTLE RIVER TP.
ALEXANDRIA
SHIRLEY HY.
VAN DORN
FRANCONIA RD.

71

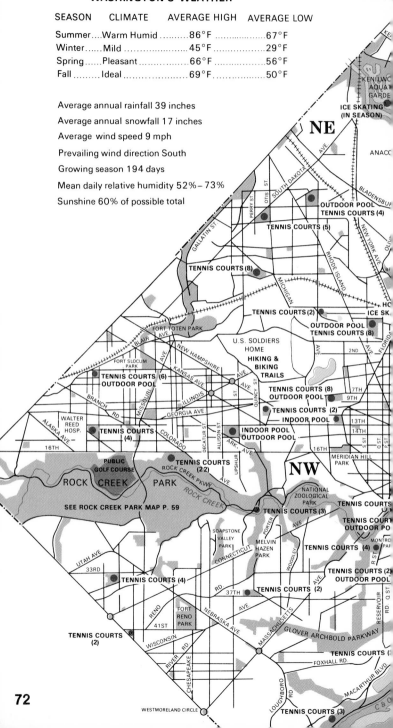

WASHINGTON'S WEATHER

SEASON	CLIMATE	AVERAGE HIGH	AVERAGE LOW
Summer	Warm Humid	86°F	67°F
Winter	Mild	45°F	29°F
Spring	Pleasant	66°F	56°F
Fall	Ideal	69°F	50°F

Average annual rainfall 39 inches

Average annual snowfall 17 inches

Average wind speed 9 mph

Prevailing wind direction South

Growing season 194 days

Mean daily relative humidity 52%–73%

Sunshine 60% of possible total

NE

KENILWO
AQUA
GARDE

ICE SKATING
(IN SEASON)

ANACO

BLADENSBU

OUTDOOR POOL
TENNIS COURTS (4)

TENNIS COURTS (5)

TENNIS COURTS (8)

TENNIS COURTS (2)

ICE SK.

OUTDOOR POOL
TENNIS COURTS (8)

FORT TOTEN PARK

U.S. SOLDIERS
HOME

HIKING &
BIKING
TRAILS

2ND

FLORIDA

HC

FORT SLOCUM
PARK

TENNIS COURTS (6)
OUTDOOR POOL

TENNIS COURTS (8)
OUTDOOR POOL

7TH
9TH

TENNIS COURTS (2)
INDOOR POOL

13TH
14TH

WALTER
REED
HOSP.

TENNIS COURTS
(4)

INDOOR POOL
OUTDOOR POOL

16TH

MERIDIAN HILL
PARK

16TH

TENNIS COURTS
(22)

NW

PUBLIC
GOLF COURSE

ROCK CREEK PKWY

NATIONAL
ZOOLOGICAL
PARK

TENNIS COURTS

ROCK CREEK PARK

SEE ROCK CREEK PARK MAP P. 59

ROCK CREEK

TENNIS COURTS (3)

TENNIS COURT
OUTDOOR PO

SOAPSTONE
VALLEY
PARK

MELVIN
HAZEN
PARK

TENNIS COURTS (4)

MONTRO
PAR

UTAH AVE.

33RD

TENNIS COURTS (4)

TENNIS COURTS (2)
OUTDOOR POOL

RESERVOIR

37TH

TENNIS COURTS (2)

FORT
RENO
PARK

RENO

41ST

NEBRASKA AVE.

GLOVER ARCHBOLD PARKWAY

TENNIS COURTS
(2)

WISCONSIN

RIVER

CHESAPEAKE

FOXHALL RD.

TENNIS COURTS (3

MACARTHUR BLVD

LOUGHBORO

WESTMORELAND CIRCLE

TENNIS COURTS (3)

SPORTS AND PARKS

← N —

● SWIMMING POOLS
 TENNIS

TENNIS COURTS (2)
OUTDOOR POOL

TENNIS COURTS (3)
OUTDOOR POOL

OUTDOOR POOL

FORT DUPONT

PUBLIC GOLF COURSE

FORT MAHAN PARK

FORT DAVIS PARK

ANACOSTIA

UBLIC GOLF COURSE

TENNIS COURTS (3)

R.F.K. STADIUM

TENNIS COURTS (2)
INDOOR POOL

OXON RUN
PUBLIC GOLF COURSE

SE

TENNIS COURTS (10)
OUTDOOR POOL
BASKETBALL
FOOTBALL
SOCCER

FORT STANTON PARK

TENNIS COURTS (3)
OUTDOOR POOL

OUTDOOR POOL

OUTDOOR POOL
INDOOR POOL

TENNIS COURTS (2)

TENNIS COURT
OUTDOOR POOL

OUTDOOR POOL

TENNIS COURTS (3)

SHEPHERD PARKWAY

OXON RUN PARKWAY

NAVAL STATION

TENNIS COURTS (2)
OUTDOOR POOL

TENNIS COURTS (2)

ICE SKATING

THE MALL

PADDLE BOAT RENTAL

WHITE HOUSE

TIDAL BASIN

WEST POTOMAC PARK

MARINA
157 SLIPS

SW

BOLLING AIR FORCE BASE

BIKE RENTAL

HAIN'S POINT

EAST POTOMAC PARK

PUBLIC GOLF COURSE
FOOTBALL
OUTDOOR POOL

TENNIS COURTS (24)

ROCHAMBEAU BRIDGE

GEORGE MASON BRIDGE

WASHINGTON NATIONAL AIRPORT

POTOMAC RIVER

SAILING MARINA
558 SLIPS

DAINGER-FIELD I.

ARLINGTON BRIDGE

COLUMBIA ISLAND MARINA
500 SLIPS

ROOSEVELT BRIDGE

THEODORE ROOSEVELT

KEY BRIDGE

HIKING

BADMINTON, CRICKET,
FOOTBALL, HOCKEY POLO,
RUGBY, SOCCER VOLLEYBALL

BIKE & CANOE RENTAL

A R L I N G T O N

© FLASHMAPS PUBLICATIONS Inc.

FOR C. & O. CANAL
SEE MAP P. 63

73

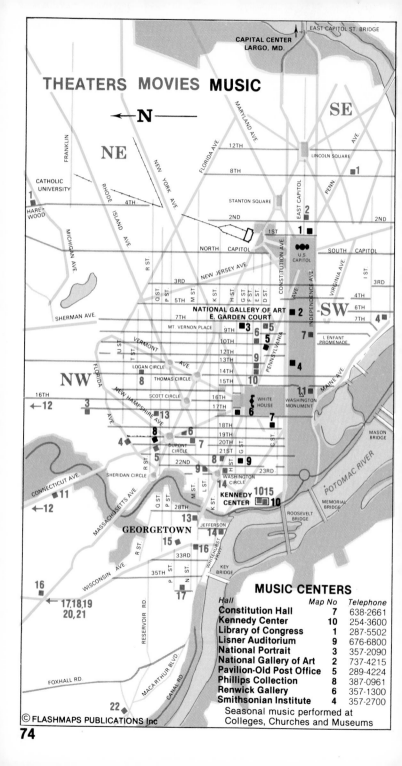

THEATERS MOVIES MUSIC

← N →

MUSIC CENTERS

Hall	Map No	Telephone
Constitution Hall	7	638-2661
Kennedy Center	10	254-3600
Library of Congress	1	287-5502
Lisner Auditorium	9	676-6800
National Portrait	3	357-2090
National Gallery of Art	2	737-4215
Pavilion-Old Post Office	5	289-4224
Phillips Collection	8	387-0961
Renwick Gallery	6	357-1300
Smithsonian Institute	4	357-2700

Seasonal music performed at
Colleges, Churches and Museums

© FLASHMAPS PUBLICATIONS Inc

THEATERS & MOVIES

THEATERS—ALPHABETICAL

Theater	Address	Map No	Telephone
Arena Stage	M & 6th St SW	4	488-3300
Carter Barron	16th & Kennedy	12	829-3200
Eisenhower	Kennedy Center	15	254-3670
Ford's	511 10th St NW	6	347-4833
Gala Hispanic	420 7th NW	5	628-2831
Hartke	Harewood NE	1	529-3333
Kreeger	M & 6th St SW	4	488-3300
Marvin Ctr GWU	800 21st St NW	14	676-4949
National	1321 Penn NW	10	628-6161
New Playwrights	1742 Church NW	13	232-1122
Old Vat Room	M & 6th St SW	4	488-3300
Olney Theater	Rte 108, Olney MD	off	*924-3400
Opera House	Kennedy Center	15	254-3770
Shakespeare	201 E Capitol	2	546-4000
Smithsonian	9th & Independence	6	287-3350
Source Co,The	1809 14th St NW	8	462-1073
Studio	1401 Church St	13	265-7412
Sylvan	The Mall	11	426-6839
Terrace Theater	Kennedy Center	15	254-9895
Trapier	Mass & Wis AveNW	16	537-6537
Trinity	36th & O St NW	17	965-4680
Warehouse Rep	1835 14th St NW	8	462-1073
Warner	513 13th St NW	9	626-1050
Wash. Proj Arts	400 7th St NW	5	347-8304

*Area (301)

—BY MAP NOS.

Map No	Theater
1	Hartke
2	Shakespeare
4	Arena Stage
4	Kreeger
4	Old Vat Rm
5	Gala Hispan
5	Wash Proj
6	Ford's
7	Smithsonian
8	Warehouse
8	Source Co
9	Warner
10	National
11	Sylvan
12	Carter Barron
13	New Playwri
13	Studio
14	Marvin GWU
15	Eisenhower
15	Opera
15	Terrace
16	Trapier
17	Trinity

MOVIES—ALPHABETICAL

Movie	Address	Map No	Telephone
Amer Film Inst	Kennedy Center	10	785-4600
Avalon I, II	5612 Conn NW	12	966-2600
Biograph	2819 M St NW	13	333-2696
Capitol Hill I, II	507 8th St SE	1	547-1210
Cerberus 1, 2, 3	3040 M St NW	14	337-1311
Cinema	5120 Wis NW	18	363-1875
Circle	2105 Penn NW	8	331-7480
Circle Uptown	3426 Conn NW	11	966-5400
Circle West End	23rd & L St NW	9	293-3152
Dupont Circle	1332 Conn NW	6	785-2300
Embassy Circle	1927 Florida NW	4	387-1344
Fine Arts	1919 M St	7	223-4438
Georgetown	1351 Wis NW	15	333-5555
Inner Circle	2105 Penn NW	8	331-7480
Janus I, 2,3	1660 Conn NW	5	232-8900
Jenifer I, II	5252 Wis NW	17	244-5703
Key	1222 Wis NW	16	333-5100
MacArthur 1, 2, 3	4859 MacArthur	22	337-1700
Ontario	1700 Columbia NW	3	667 1058
Outer Circle I, II	4849 Wis NW	19	244-3116
Paris	5300 Wisconsin	18	686-7700
Studio I, II, III	4600 Wis NW	20	686-1700
Tenley Circle I-III	4200 Wis NW	21	363-4340

—BY MAP NOS.

Map No	Theater
1	Capitol
3	Ontario
4	Embassy Cir
5	Janus 1, 2, 3
6	Dupont Cir
7	Fine Arts
8	Circle
8	Inner Cir
9	Cir West End
10	Amer Film Inst
11	Cir Uptown
12	Avalon I,II
13	Biograph
14	Cerberus 1-3
15	Georgetown
16	Key
17	Jenifer I, II
18	Cinema
18	Paris
19	Outer Circle
20	Studio
21	Tenley Circle
22	MacArthur

Wolf Trap Farm   1624 Trap Rd, Vienna, VA 255-1800   (see page 61)

MUSEUMS—ART • HISTORY • SCIENCE

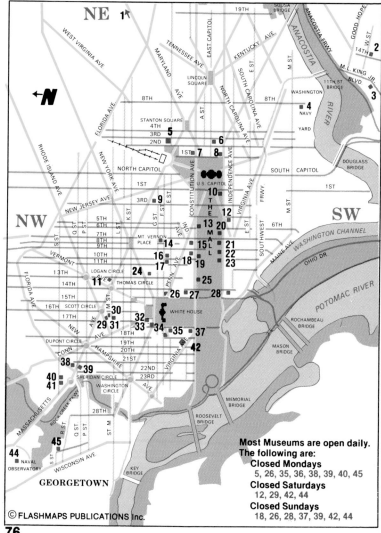

NE

NW   SW

Most Museums are open daily.
The following are:

Closed Mondays
5, 26, 35, 36, 38, 39, 40, 45

Closed Saturdays
12, 29, 42, 44

Closed Sundays
18, 26, 28, 37, 39, 42, 44

GEORGETOWN

© FLASHMAPS PUBLICATIONS Inc.

MUSEUMS—ART • HISTORY • SCIENCE

Museum	Address	Weekday Hours ★	Map No.	Telephone
African, Near East, Asia	The Mall	10-5:30	22	357-2700
Air & Space Museum	The Mall	10-5:30	20	357-2700
Anacostia Neighborhood	2405 Martin L King	10-6	3	287-3369
Anderson House	2118 Mass NW	1-4	39	785-0540
Arts & Industries Building	The Mall	10-5:30	22	357-2700
Bethune Archives	1318 Vermont Ave NW	10-4:30	11	332-1233
B'nai B'rith Klutznick	1640 Rhode Island NW	10-5	29	857-6583
Botanic Gardens	The Mall	9-4	10	225-8333
Bureau Engraving, Printing	14th & NC St SW	8-2	28	566-2000
Capitol, The	The Mall	9-3	10	225-6827
Children's Museum	800 3rd St, NE	10-4	5	543-8600
Contemporary Latin Amer Art	201 18th St NW	10-5	37	789-6019
Corcoran Gallery	17th & New York NW	10-4:30	35	638-3211
DAR Museum	1776 D St NW	9-4	35	628-1776
Decatur, Stephen House	740 Jackson Place	10-2	32	673-4030
Dept of Interior	C & Virginia Ave, NW	8-4	42	343-2743
Dolls' & Toy Museum	5236 44th St, NW	10-5	off	244-0024
Dumbarton Oaks/Gardens	1703 32nd St NW	2-5	45	338-8278
Federal Bur Investigation	Penn & 9th St NW	9-4:15	18	324-3000
Folger Shakespeare Library	201 E Capitol	10-4:30	6	544-4600
Ford's Theater	511 10th St NW	9-5	16	426-6924
Frederick Douglass Home	14th & W St SE	9-4	2	426-5960
Freer Gallery	The Mall	10-5:30	23	357-2700
Hillwood Museum	4155 Linnean Ave NW	by app't	off	686-5807
Hirshhorn Mus & Sculpture	The Mall	10-5:30	21	357-2700
Howard Univ Art Gallery	2455 6th Street, NW	9-4	off	636-7070
Jewish Historical Society	701 Third St. NW	Sunday	9	789-0900
Library of Congress	Independence & 1st SE	8:30-9	8	287-5000
Marine Corps Historic Ctr	9th & M SE (Navy Yd)	10-4	4	433-3534
Museum of Natural History	The Mall	10-5:30	19	357-2700
National American History	The Mall	10-5:30	25	357-2700
National Aquarium	14th & E St NW	9-5	27	377-2825
National Arboretum	See page 58	8-5	1	475-4815
National Archives	Constitution & 8th SE	10-6	15	523-3216
National Building Mus	441 F St NW	10-4	9	272-2448
National Gallery of Art	The Mall	10-5	13	737-4215
Nat'l Geographic Explorers	17th & M St NW	9-6	31	857-7588
National Firearms Museum	Rhode Island & 16th	10-4	30	828-6194
Nat'l Mus Women in the Arts	801 13th Street NW	10-5	24	337-2615
National Zoo	3000 Conn (see pg 60)	9-4:30	off	673-4800
Naval Observatory	Mass & 34th St NW	2:00	44	653-1543
Navy, The	9th & MSE (Navy Yd)	9-4	4	433-2651
Octagon House	1799 New York NW	10-4	36	638-3105
Peterson House (LINCOLN DIED)	516 10th St NW	9-5	17	426-6830
Phillips Collection	1600 21st St NW	10-5	38	387-2151
Portrait Gllry/Mus Amer Art	G St & 8th NW	10-5:30	14	357-2700
Renwick Gallery	Penn & 17th St NW	10-5:30	34	357-2700
Sewall-Belmont House	144 Constitution NE	10-5	7	546-3989
Textile Museum	2320 S St NW	10-5	40	667-0441
White House	1600 Pennsylvania NW	10-12	26	456-7041
Woodrow Wilson House	2340 S St NW	10-2	41	673-4034
Voice of America	330 Independence SW	9-4	12	485-6231

★ **Hours vary Saturday, Sunday & Summer months**

WASHINGTON SUBURBS

Community/Population	Approx Miles Center DC	Routes to Area	Nearest Beltway Exit ★
Alexandria, VA (103,217)	6	Route 1	1
Andrews AFB, MD (10,064)	10	Route 4 & 5	7-11
Annadale, VA (49,524)	12.5	Little River or Columbia Pike	6
Arlington ,VA (152,599)	5	Arlington Blvd	8
Beltsville, MD (12,760)	8.5	Route 1	25
Berwyn Heights, MD (3,135)	12	Routes 201 & 1	23
Bethesda, MD (62,736)	8	Wisconsin Ave	34
Bladensburg, MD (7,691)	6.5	Bladensburg Rd	17, 20
Bowie, MD (33,695)	15	John Hanson Hwy (Rt. 50)	19
Capitol Heights, MD (3,271)	6.5	Central Ave (Rt. 332)	15
Cheverly, MD (5,751)	6.5	John Hanson Hwy (Rt. 50)	19
Chevy Chase, MD (12,232)	6	Wisconsin or Conn Avenues	33, 34
College Park, MD (23,624)	7	Route 1	25, 23
Crystal City, VA	4	Route 1	1
District Heights, MD (6,799)	7	Marlboro Pike	11
Fairfax, VA (19,390)	15	Little River Turnpike	6
Falls Church, VA (9,515)	8	Lee Highway	8, 9
Fort Belvoir, VA (7,726)	15	Route 1	1
Friendship Heights, MD	6	Wisconsin Ave	34
Gaithersburg, MD (26,424)	20	Wash Natl Pike (Rt. 270)	38, 34
Glen Echo, MD (229)	8	Mass Ave or MacArthur Blvd	41, 39
Glendale, MD (5,106)	13	Georgetown Pike (Rt. 193)	13
Greenbelt, MD (17,332)	12	Baltimore Wash Pkwy (Rt. 1)	22
Herndon, VA (11,449)	20	Leesburg Hwy (Rt. 7)	11, 12
Hillcrest Heights, MD (17,021)	7.5	Branch Ave (Rt. 5)	7
Hollywood, MD	11	Route 1	25
Hyattsville, MD (12,709)	7	Rhode Island Ave (Rt. 1)	23, 25
Kensington, MD (1,822)	8.5	Connecticut Ave	33
Kenwood, MD	6.5	River Road	39
Laurel, MD (12,103)	16	Baltimore Wash Pkwy (Rt. 1)	25
Leisure World, MD	15	Georgia Ave (Rt. 97)	31
Lewisdale, MD	7	Route 212	25
McLean, VA (35,664)	8.5	Route 123	11
Merrifield, VA (7,525)	10	Lee Highway	8, 9
Mt. Rainier, MD (7,361)	5.5	Queens Chapel Rd	25
Mt. Vernon, VA (24,058)	13	Washington Mem Hwy (Rt. 1)	1
Oxon Hill, MD (36,267)	9	Indian Head (Rt. 210)	3
Reston, VA (36,407)	18	Leesburg Pike (Rt. 7)	11, 12
Rockville, MD (43,811)	15	Rockville Pike (Rt. 355)	34
Seat Pleasant, MD (5,217)	7.5	Route 704	15, 17
Silver Spring, MD (72,893)	7	Route 29	29, 36
Somerset, MD (1,101)	6.5	Wisconsin Avenue	34
Springfield, VA (21,435)	12	Shirley Hwy (Rt. 95)	4
Suitland, MD (32,164)	6.5	Route 218	7
Takoma Park, MD (16,231)	6	Georgia Ave & Piney Branch	30, 29
Tremont, VA	9	Arlington Blvd (Rt. 50)	8
Tyson's Corner, VA (10,065)	10	Dolly Madison & Leesburg Pk	10, 11
Wheaton, MD (48,598)	10	Georgia Ave (Rt. 97)	31
Vienna, VA (15,469)	13	Route 123	10, 11
White Oak, Md (13,700)	11	Route 29	28-30

★ Beltway Map page 6

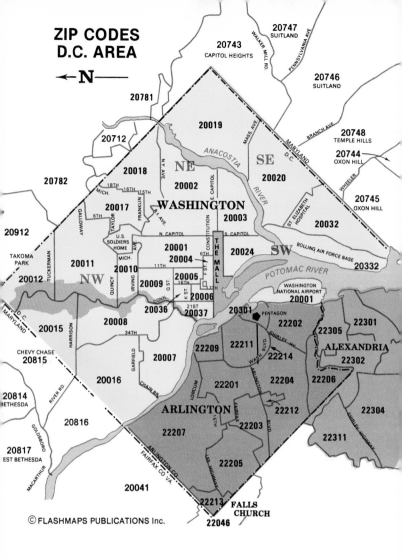

ZIP CODES
D.C. AREA
← N →

20747 SUITLAND

20743 CAPITOL HEIGHTS

20781

20746 SUITLAND

20712

20748 TEMPLE HILLS

20019

20744 OXON HILL

20782

20018

NE

SE

20002

20020

20745 OXON HILL

20912

20017

WASHINGTON

20003

TAKOMA PARK

U.S. SOLDIERS HOME

20001

20024

SW

20032

20011

20004

THE MALL

BOLLING AIR FORCE BASE

20012

NW

20010

20005

20332

20015

20009

20006

POTOMAC RIVER

WASHINGTON NATIONAL AIRPORT

20036

20008

20037

20301

20001

CHEVY CHASE
20815

20007

PENTAGON

22202

22301

20814 BETHESDA

20016

22209

22211

22214

22305

ALEXANDRIA

22302

20817 EST BETHESDA

20816

22201

22204

22206

22304

ARLINGTON

22212

22207

22203

22311

20041

22205

22213 FALLS CHURCH

© FLASHMAPS PUBLICATIONS Inc.

22046

General Post Office - N Capitol & M assachusetts Ave - 7am to midnight
Main Post Office - 200 Brentwood Rd NE - 8am to 8pm

ZIP CODE INFORMATION:

523-2375 - weekdays 7:00 am to 12 pm

The White House	20500
The Senate	20510
House of Representatives	20515
The Supreme Court	20543

GLOSSARY

English	French	German	Italian	Spanish
Architecture	Architecture	Architektur	Architettura	Arquitectura
Art	Art	Kunst	Arte	Arte
Buses	Autobus	Autobusse	Autobus	Autobus
Churches	Eglises	Kirchen	Chiese	Iglesias
Colleges	Universites	Universitaten	Universita'	Universidades
Embassies	Ambassades	Botschaften	Ambasciate	Embajadas
Emergency Numbers	Numeros d'urgence	Notnummern	Numeri d'emergenza	Numeros de Emergencia
Galleries	Galleries	Gallerien	Gallerie	Galeria
History	Histoire	Geschichte	Storia	Istoria
Highways	Grandes Routes	Landstrassen	Autostrade	Carreteras
Hospitals	Hopitaux	Krakenhauser	Ospedali	Hospital
Hotels	Hctels	Hotels	Hotel	Hotel
Libraries	Biblioteques	Bibliotheken	Biblioteche	Bibliotecas
Museums	Musees	Museen	Musei	Museos
Music	Musique	Musik	Musica	Musica
Movies	Cinemas	Filme	Cinema	Peliculas
Parks	Parcs	Parks	Giardini Publici	Parques
Restaurants	Restaurants	Restaurants	Ristoranti	Restaurantes
Science	Science	Wissenschaft	Scienze	Ciencia
Shops	Grands Magasins	Einkaufen	Negozi	Negocios
Sports	Sports	Sport	Sport	Desportes
Subways	Metro	Untergrundbahnen	Metropolitana	Subterraneo
Taxi	Taxi	Taxi	Tassi'	Taxi
Theaters	Theatres	Theater	Teatri	Teatros
Zoo	Zoo	Zoo	Zoo	Jardin Zoologicc

FLASHMAPS Instant Guides
Available From Your
Local Bookseller:

New York   **Los Angeles**
Washington DC   **San Francisco**
Chicago   **Boston**
Dallas/Ft Worth   **Philadelphia**

MAKES A CITY FEEL HOMETOWN™